Planting Churches – Changing Communities

'David's book will be a great encouragement to anybody pondering the possibility of starting a new church. Full of biblically-based wisdom and practical insights, it is made more colourful by the inclusion of many testimonies from contemporary church planters who write honestly and instructively about their experiences ... I would add that those leading established churches should also read this very motivational book, because when you abandon an atmosphere of aggressive evangelism and commitment to growth you are actually signing up for stagnation and death. Every small group leader in an existing church would find fresh energy and provocation by reading it.'

Terry Virgo, *Newfrontiers*

'David writes on this subject, about which he's passionate, with great clarity and considerable authority. Not only does he talk about church planting; he's actually done it, several times and with great success. So, if you're at all interested in church planting, sell your shirt to buy this book – it'll probably become a classic!'

John Mumford,
National Director of Vineyard Movement in the UK

'At a time when many critics are declaring that the church in Britain will soon disappear, why would anyone write a manual on church planting? The answer's simple. The greatest thing that could happen to renew the nation's soul and reverse it's frightening decline, is the launch of effective new churches everywhere, churches that are Gospel-centred, spiritually alive, compassionate, highly relational, community transforming and able to heal their towns and cities with something that's real and not fake.

David Stroud has written an immensely clear, readable and practical guide on how to build great churches from scratch. He's thought of just about everything we need to know, in a book that will help missional churches everywhere to prioritise what's closest to Christ's heart, namely the recovery and rescue of hope-less people so they can become truly human again in relationship with Christ and with others. This book is a God-send.'

Greg Haslam, Minister, Westminster Chapel, London.

'Fantastic! At last a manual that deals with the issues of Church Planting and how to grow a fellowship written by a man with hands on experience. I have admired David's vision, tenacity and gifting for many years and I believe any individual or church with a heart to see the Kingdom of God increased should not only read but apply the principles laid out.'

Revd Dr David E Carr, Senior Minister Renewal Christian Centre

'Planting churches is one thing but planting churches which leave traces of the Kingdom of God which transforms communities is someting else altogether. That's what this is!'

Joel Edwards, International Director of Micah Challenge

'Every Christian should be involved in church planting. This book is a valuable resource, whether you are called to support others as they go, help recapture something of the energy of a plant in an existing church, go yourself as part of a team, or even lead a brand new church. Throughout the book church planters share stories about what it is really like to start churches.

Dave Stroud is a wise master builder and shares practical insights, which answer questions such as: How do churches start? How do I know if I should go on a church plant? What qualities does a church plant leader need?

Read this book with an open heart and it will help you discover what God wants you to do to help re-evangelize our world.'

Adrian Warnock, blogger, adrianwarnock.com

'David Stroud has succeeded in combining a great vision for starting many new churches with effective and well-proven strategies for turning this vision into reality by the Holy Spirit's power. I commend this book to all who are involved in church planting and Christian leadership generally.'

David Devenish, *Newfrontiers*

Planting Churches –
Changing Communities

*A hands-on guide to successful
church planting*

David Stroud

Authentic

MILTON KEYNES • COLORADO SPRINGS • HYDERABAD

15 14 13 12 11 10 09   7 6 5 4 3 2 1

This edition first published 2009 by Authentic Media
9 Holdom Avenue, Bletchley, Milton Keynes, Bucks, MK1 1QR, UK
1820 Jet Stream Drive, Colorado Springs, CO 80921, USA
Medchal Road, Jeedimetla Village, Secunderabad 500 055, AP, India
www.authenticmedia.co.uk

Authentic Media is a division of IBS-STL UK, limited by guarantee, with
its Registered Office at Kingstown Broadway, Carlisle, Cumbria CA3 0HA.
Registered in England & Wales No. 1216232. Registered charity 270162

British Library Cataloguing in Publication Data
A catalogue record for this book is available from the British Library

ISBN 13: 978-1-85078-856-0

Cover design by David Smart
Print Management by Adare
Typeset by Waverley Typesetters, Fakenham
Printed and bound in the UK by J.F. Print Ltd., Sparkford, Somerset

To Steve Nicholson, for igniting a passion for church planting in my heart.

To Philippa, thank you for coming on the journey with me. I cannot imagine having travelled with another. Thank you for doing so with such love and being so ready to sacrifice when needed.

To Edward, Victoria and Rebekah, the best church planting team I could have ever asked for.

CONTENTS

Section 3: The planting phase

FOREWORD

Church planting, it has been observed, is the most effective form of evangelism. Some statisticians have done the sums and worked out that you get more individuals saved through church planting than from any other form of evangelism. Sadly, however, by simply adding up the numbers they are in danger of missing the point.

Church planting is not simply a matter of getting a number of individuals saved; it is about the advance of God's community in the earth. He wants a community, his city, his family in which he could dwell. Church planting is an extension of the community, not simply an exercise in multiplying the head count. Part of God's purpose in saving us is to overcome our intense selfishness and isolation.

This community then becomes the place where God is manifested on the earth. His people are his dwelling place where he can be found and encountered. There is no need to make a pilgrimage to a designated holy place, be it Jerusalem or Mecca. God's people are his holy dwelling. God is accessible on his planet among his people. So when we plant a church in a new location, we are establishing a temple where God can be encountered, where his presence is felt and experienced. Holy lifestyles, lived out in holy communities, replace holy relics and historic locations.

God wants a wonderful family growing throughout the world; a place where lives are changed; where his presence is felt and lost people can find a home. Starting churches then is at the very heart of God's mission here on earth.

David's book will be a great encouragement to anybody pondering the possibility of starting a new church. Full of Biblically-based wisdom and practical insights, it is made more colourful by the inclusion of many testimonies from contemporary church planters who write honestly and instructively about their experiences.

This is a first rate guide carrying within its pages an attitude of faith and expectation of ultimate success and the inevitability of gospel advance through robust church planting. The challenges and difficulties are not hidden but are approached with genuine answers and accumulated wisdom gathered by many who have trod this path with success.

Some of us have found help and inspiration from dipping into books written in the USA. It is exciting to be able to recommend a British-based book, rooted in British experience, written essentially for British readers, though any who read it will find inspiration.

I would add that those leading established churches should also read this very motivational book, because when you abandon an atmosphere of aggressive evangelism and commitment to growth you are actually signing up for stagnation and death. Every small group leader in an existing church would find fresh energy and provocation by reading it.

TERRY VIRGO
Newfrontiers

ACKNOWLEDGEMENTS

This book has definitely been a team effort and I want to express my appreciation to everyone who has had a hand in it.

Howard Kellett has gathered the various church planting stories, added quotes and Scripture references to the text and given his comments and thoughts as we have gone along. Adam James has tirelessly made himself available to cover every loose end. Liz Brown has checked the references and compiled the endnotes. Andy Moyle wrote the mission, vision and values worksheet. Paul Mogford advised and helped me along the way. I am deeply grateful to each of them for the energy they have given to this project and the way they have responded, often facing very tight deadlines.

Thank you too, to all the church planters (listed overleaf) who gave their time to be interviewed and shared their stories and insights. Their contributions have brought this material to life.

THUMBNAIL BIOGRAPHIES OF CONTRIBUTORS

Colin Baron began his church planting journey when he moved to lead a church plant into Swanley, North Kent. In 1994 Colin and Mary moved to Manchester and pioneered multiple church plants across the region. After a short time in New England, USA, Colin is now planting a church in the East of Manchester.

Jonathan and Helen Bell moved to Birmingham in 1996 in order to plant Churchcentral. Prior to that Jonathan spent four years on the staff of The Vine Church in Odiham, Hampshire.

Matthew and Ann Clifton-Brown planted their first church in Newcastle in 1986 with Ian and Heather Galloway. Matthew was a social worker at the time. They subsequently moved to plant King's Church in Edinburgh in 2002.

David Coak worked in the building industry for twenty years, then led the Haywards Heath church which began under Terry Virgo's guidance in 1977. In 1993 David and Margaret moved to Cambridge to church plant and then again in 2005 to plant in Oxford.

Pete Cornford trained as a teacher in London where he met his wife Nicky. Pete was a Pastoral Assistant with David Holden in Sidcup, then served on the staff of Beacon Church, Camberley, before moving back to London in 2002 to plant The Crown Church in Hillingdon.

Stu and Livy Gibbs joined a church plant in Bristol when they were students and stayed for nine years before moving to plant in Greenwich in November 2007. Emmanuel Church, London, went public in September 2008.

Duncan Hanton moved to London as a student. After working for the BBC and a Latin American missionary organisation, he served on the staff of Queens Road Church, Wimbledon. In 2003 Duncan and Jill moved to Mill Hill, London, to plant Northwest Church.

Matt Hatch joined the staff of King's Arms, Bedford, after graduating from university. Matt later led King's Arms. Matt and his wife Pip then moved to Leeds and planted Mosaic Church in October 2004.

Dave and Gill Harper started Church in the Peak in their home in the late 1980s. Church in the Peak now meets in Matlock and from this base church, other churches have now been planted out into Buxton and Chesterfield.

Anthony Henson, who is married to Gill, was as elder at Sidcup before planting into Orpington, Leicester and Stoke-on-Trent. During this time three other church planting teams were sent out from these churches. Anthony and Gill are currently leading a relatively new church plant in Lincoln.

Howard Kellett worked as a teacher for fourteen years before serving for four years as an evangelist at King's Church, Catford. In 2001 Howard and his wife Naomi moved north to plant Hope Church, Manchester.

Chris Kilby was a creative arts teacher for ten years before joining the staff of Winchester Family Church with Greg Haslam. He then served as an evangelist and elder there with John Groves until 2007, when he and his wife Jo moved their family to central Southampton to plant Life Southampton.

Mark Landreth-Smith worked on the staff of the Coign Church, Woking, before he and his wife Bev moved to Camberley to plant the Beacon Church.

Stef Liston was saved in Dartford and later attended and served on the staff of City Hope Church, Bermondsey. Stef and his wife Davina are currently planting Revelation Church in Camden, North London.

Andy Moyle met his wife Janet on a year team in Sunderland before becoming a church youth worker. He planted The Bridge Church, St Ives, in 2001 and is now planting The Gateway Church in King's Lynn.

Steve Petch originally trained as a pharmacist and pursued that career for over ten years. He was an elder in King's Church, Horsham, before planting Billingshurst Family Church in 2001. Steve and Jo moved to plant Grace Church, Chichester in 2006.

Chris Vincent was a science teacher before serving on the staff of Brickhill Church, Bedford. In 1995 Chris and Rachel led a successful church plant into Chelmsford before

God dramatically called them to plant Saoirse Church in Dublin, in 2007.

Tony Thompson worked in industry for eleven years before joining the staff of Brickhill Baptist Church where he worked as an evangelist. He left in 1994 to plant Open Door Church in St Neots. He moved again in 2002 to start Hope Church in Luton. Tony is married to Anne who is a head teacher.

Martin White moved to Bedford to do a year team and then stayed on to be involved in planting the King's Arms. In 1998 he and his wife Louise moved to plant The Crown, Handsworth, an intentionally multicultural church in a diverse, inner city borough of Birmingham.

INTRODUCTION

> 'I will build my church, and the gates of Hades will not overcome it.'
>
> Matthew 16:18

A Ghanaian pastor took the microphone at our summer conference and spoke words that totally changed our approach to church planting. His prophetic words were these: 'God says, "I want you to believe me for 1,000 churches in this nation."'

At the time, the leadership of *Newfrontiers* were working slowly towards 200 churches, so his words sent us reeling. Could this possibly be God speaking to us? We hesitated, awed by the enormity of the challenge and yet were drawn by the sense that this really was God's voice.

Our plans for 200 churches were something that we thought we could achieve. God's plans suddenly seemed so much bigger! But that, we reflected, is often the mark of God's plans: he calls us to do things that are impossible unless he is in them.

This manual has been written out of the conviction that if we are to start hundreds of new churches, then there is value in distilling down into one volume some of what we have learnt over the last twenty years, whilst planting churches up and down the UK.

My hope is that it will not just be read by *Newfrontiers* church planters, but by others as well. We will certainly need churches started from all sorts of backgrounds if this nation is going to feel the impact of a resurgent church and realise that God is alive amongst his people.

This handbook has been written with some underlying convictions:

1. *The church is the hope of the world.* There is nothing else so close to God's heart or with so much nation-changing potential as the local church.

2. *Many more churches planted will enable God's people to play a greater role in changing this nation* – through evangelism, care for the poor, social justice and cultural transformation. In other words, as we see more and more people come to Christ and more and more leaders trained, so it will give God's people greater 'reach' to have an effect on their culture, to be the 'salt and light' that Jesus has called us to be.

3. More churches planted in this nation will result in a *new wave of men and women who will go to the ends of the earth and contribute to a new missions movement* that will touch many nations.

What this handbook is

This handbook is a practical manual full of examples that have worked in real life church planting situations. The material here will enable church planters to work out what they need to do and what skills they need to develop in order to be effective and to plant more churches in less time than they would do otherwise.

It is not a book of theology. It is not that theology is not important. On the contrary, it is essential. All church planters should gain a thorough, working systematic theology which will undergird their preaching, inform their living and shape their church planting. There are lots of great resources available to help them to do this and *Newfrontiers* runs many courses that equip people in this way. This book, however, is not covering that ground, but rather concentrating on what needs to be done.

How to use this handbook

This manual can be read from cover to cover or dipped into wherever it looks like it will be most interesting or most helpful. I have tried to keep the fine balance between offering practical, do-able suggestions and being over-prescriptive. The advantage of what is written here is that it has worked in live situations up and down the UK in recent years. However, I realise that each situation is different and that each church planter needs to hear from the Spirit as to how to apply biblical principles in each situation. Therefore I encourage you to handle this material prayerfully and with an ear open to the Spirit at all times.

Alongside this handbook there is also a website: www.ukchurchplanting.org where you will find further resources, including interviews with seasoned church planters, a list of all current *Newfrontiers* church plants and details of forthcoming conferences and training events.

Content that has been tried and found to work

As you read through these pages you will find quotes and stories from leaders who have planted churches in different parts of the UK in recent years. These have been included to show how the principles have been applied in real situations by real people. This is not simply material that works in theory; it has been road tested in numerous situations and has been proven to work.

You will find that most of the quotes are sourced. However, a few are anonymous to protect an individual's privacy where necessary.

Some comments on terminology

I have tried to keep technical terminology to a minimum and where possible use terms that are found within Scripture. One exception to this is the use of 'small group'. I use this to describe the groups that most churches have midweek in venues other than the one used for its main worship services. All sorts of terms are currently used for these groups including cell groups, life groups and house groups. I have used 'small group' as a catch-all term to describe whichever of these other terms a church plant is using.

For God's glory

The biggest drawback to focusing so much on the practical side of church planting is that there is a danger of forgetting the primary motivation for starting churches: to bring great glory to Jesus Christ.

It is because of what Jesus has done, and with the desire that his fame will spread, that this book has been written.

I pray that as you use this handbook it will stimulate you, motivate you and inspire you to get on with planting churches for God's glory across this nation and the nations until he returns.

DAVID STROUD
April 2009

Section 1:
The preparation phase

1

WHY PLANT CHURCHES?

> 'Nothing else — not crusades, outreach programs, para-church ministries, growing mega-churches, congregational consulting, nor church renewal processes — will have the consistent impact of dynamic, extensive church planting.'[1]
>
> Tim Keller and J. Allen Thompson

I had no idea how deeply my heart would be affected by spending a few months in Chicago. My host, Steve Nicholson, was passionately committed to planting churches. He picked me up from the airport and his passion overflowed immediately: 'Do you know the single greatest bottleneck to us planting more churches across this nation?' he asked as we drove away from the airport. I confessed that I had no idea. 'Leaders,' he replied. 'We have got plenty of people who want to be part of a church planting team, but we do not have enough leaders to get them going.' These were new ideas to me, but I found myself thinking, 'If there is this sort of lack in God's church then maybe I should let God know that I am available – if he really thinks he can use me!'

I found myself talking with Steve about his great love of starting churches on many occasions over the next few months. As we did so, I started to understand just how central it was to God's purposes and why it should demand so much of my time and energy over the coming years.

I went on to start churches in Bedford (the King's Arms), Birmingham (Oasis Church) and London (ChristChurch London), whilst also training, supporting and helping many others to do the same in other parts of the UK. Currently the *Newfrontiers* UK team, which I lead, is overseeing the planting of approximately one church every month.

It is, in my opinion, one of the most exciting ventures we can possibly be involved in as we serve God's purposes on earth and one that I believe is of great importance for the body of Christ.

In this section we look at a number of reasons for this:

- Church planting matters to God because he has always been focused on having a people for himself. Since the call of Abraham, God has made it clear that he wants to glorify himself through a people (Gen. 12:1–3).

  His people are the church. When it is functioning as it should do, the church demonstrates what an amazing, powerful, supernatural entity it is. It shows how very different groups of people can love each other and how normal people can live in a way that speaks of an entirely different value system (John 13:35; Eph. 2:15,22; Col. 3:1–14). It shows what men and women can do when they are filled with God's Spirit and believing him for impact in their communities (e.g. Acts 19).

  The church is God's passion (Eph. 5:25) so it must be ours as well. We should gain great joy

'God's intention has always been to glorify himself through building communities of people who will glorify him.'[2]

Stanley Grenz
Theology for the Community of God

from co-working with him to start new churches wherever we can.

- Jesus clearly anticipated that evangelism and church planting would go together.

  Winning the lost naturally involves 'baptising them' (Matt. 28:19), which implies involvement in the local church.

  In Acts we see this worked out as evangelism and church planting go hand in hand. When 3,000 people came to Christ on the day of Pentecost they were immediately 'added' to the other 120 who were already believers. This pattern of conversion and then being connected to existing believers continues throughout the book (for instance Acts 4:4; 6:7; 9:31; 16:5).

- Church planting is the best tool for making disciples (Matt. 28:18–20).

  Jesus did not charge us with simply winning converts, but making disciples.

  Disciples are made in the crucible of the local church. It is in this context that we learn to respond well to leadership, serve consistently and deal with our sin and weaknesses.

It is, therefore, in the process of winning people to Christ and building them into the church that we obey the Great Commission to 'make disciples' who can then reproduce themselves in others and so continue the disciple-making cycle.

• New churches grow more quickly than old ones.

Church plants are much better at focusing on evangelism than existing churches. They know why they have started (to reach the lost) and live with a sense of urgency to get on with the job. Apart from anything else, they know that if they do not become effective at reaching the lost then they will probably not exist in a couple of years time!

'When Helen and I moved to Birmingham we only knew two people in the whole city. This focused our minds somewhat! If the church was going to be planted we had to get to know as many unbelievers as possible ... and fast! We set up a Neighbourhood Watch scheme on our road; joined the local gym; I started playing for a local football team; you name it, we tried it. However, our first real breakthrough came through a completely unexpected channel. A friend of a friend got chatting about Jesus to one of their Birmingham-based lawyer friends. To cut a long story short, within two months of arriving in the city we ended up running an Alpha Course in our home with six lawyers we'd previously never met. Better still, four of them became Christians! I still remember Nathan starting to speak in tongues on the Holy Spirit day — he'd never even heard of the gift of tongues before and there he was praising Jesus in another language in the middle of our lounge!'

Jonathan Bell, Churchcentral, Birmingham

More churches are needed in the UK. If there was a move of God in the UK there would not be enough churches for a significant proportion of the population to attend. So, new churches help us prepare for what we believe God wants to do in this land.

- Churches are more effective at accomplishing God's purposes than lots of isolated individuals (Acts 19:17–27).

   Disciples working together have a lot more resources and 'reach' than they would if they were simply working by themselves. This is one of the most important implications of Paul's teaching that we are to be a body, all working together (1 Cor. 12:12–31).

- Churches that release people to be involved in church planting are more likely to be healthy churches.

   Many churches are not growing numerically and will stagnate if they do not send people out (including leaders) to be involved in the starting of new churches.

   This is a great thing to do. It is invariably a step of faith but one that God consistently honours.

'Give, and it will be given to you. A good measure, pressed down, shaken together and running over, will be poured into your lap. For with the measure you use, it will be measured to you.'

Luke 6:38

'I remember the first time one of my leaders came to me to say that he felt God had spoken to him about going to plant a church. I was absolutely devastated! It was not that I doubted God was speaking to him, but more that I could not see how we would manage without this gifted leader and elder. For some time, everything I did was dominated by this single thought: "How on earth am I going to cope without him?"

I was amazed to find that after he left others stepped up and filled the gaps he had left very quickly. Within six months we were functioning just as well as when he was with us, but now a new church was going to be started and other leaders had grown to fill his place. As I looked back on the whole process I was able to see that when you release those who God is calling to start a church, then everyone gets to grow and everyone gets to play a part in taking the kingdom forward!'[2]

Anonymous

'I had always been involved in church life, but getting involved in a church plant took my own experience and learning curve to a whole new level. In particular, the increased responsibility that came with knowing, "If I don't do this, it might not happen," was really good for me. It helped me realise that leadership is more about character than simply gifting and the church planting environment helped me develop that in abundance. I'm more reliant on God as a result, more able to show initiative and take risks.'

Andy Tilsley, member of the ChristChurch London church planting team

Sometime during 2007 it is estimated that the population of the world became more than 50% urban. Currently 70 million people a year are moving to the cities. That is roughly ten cities the size of London being created every year. The UN estimates that this will continue until there is an equilibrium of around 80% of the world living in cities, 20% in the countryside.[3]

- Church planting produces growing Christians.

  When healthy Christians go church planting they grow more. This is because they so often find themselves in challenging situations. They are no longer able to rely on others with more experience, but have to take things on themselves.

- More churches are needed across the world.

  Whilst this handbook is primarily focused on the UK, it is important to bear in mind the global need as well.

  Globally, the world's population is growing at an incredible rate (over the next 40 years the world population will grow by a third to reach 9.1 billion by 2050).*

  To keep pace with this increase we must start many new churches.

  This population growth is almost entirely to be found in cities and particularly in the cities of the developing world. This means that the cities of the world must be a particular focus of a new wave of intentional church planting.

If you are to be involved in planting churches then you must live with the conviction that this is something that is essential for God's plans and purposes. This will energise and strengthen you to do whatever you can to contribute to God's great cause. It also raises a question: what particular role do you have to play? Is God calling you to be involved in church planting personally? It is to this question that we now focus our attention.

---

* See UN Press Release POP/918 (24/02/2005): http://www.un.org/News/Press/docs/2005/pop918.doc.htm.

2

THE CALL OF A CHURCH PLANTER

'Then I heard the voice of the Lord saying, "Whom shall we send? And who will go for us?" And I said, "Here am I. Send me!"'

Isaiah 6:8

'God made me fast. And when I run, I feel his pleasure.'

Eric Liddell
400m Gold Medallist, 1924 Paris Olympics;
missionary to China

'Don't go church planting without being sure of a call from God,' was the advice I received as a sixth former who was starting to consider whether I would eventually serve the Lord in a full time context.

It was not the advice I was expecting when I walked into the Religious Education lesson that morning, but somehow we got onto the subject of calling and my teacher, who was a Christian, put it like this: 'David, only work full time for the church if the sense of God's call is so strong you can do nothing else!'

This was great advice. It is also just as relevant for today's would-be church planters as it was for me back then.

The first time I felt God's call to plant a church it came out of a deep sense of compassion and longing for people in the centre of my hometown, Bedford. I found myself highly charged and motivated to reach out and see people come to Christ and have their lives transformed. This was something that developed over a period of ten years or so, starting when I was a teenager. I would often feel God tugging at my heart when I was shopping or meeting with friends in the town centre. A trip into town could easily end up as a time of evangelism or leave me praying that God would change people's lives.

Having led the church I started in Bedford for just over five years, I unexpectedly felt God speaking to me again. I went to a meeting with some men who had apostolic and prophetic ministries and during the course of the meeting one of them leaned forward in his chair and challenged me, 'I think you should move to Birmingham!'

This gave Philippa and I a lot of thinking to do! As we reflected on the challenge we had been given we knew that we had a passion for cities, but also realised that we had something of a call too. Significantly, David Devenish, my pastor at the time, had once taken me aside and told me that he felt that God wanted me to spend much of my life working in cities.

To our surprise, my fellow elders at the King's Arms also felt this was from God and so, after further thought and discussion, we decided to make the move.

In contrast, the sense of call to go to London had started many years before when I was in my late teens. I was on a train coming out of Waterloo station when God spoke to me and said, 'One day you are to come back here and start churches.' Twenty years later a family member challenged us to make the move and this was followed by God speaking to us in some remarkable ways that resulted in us moving into the Capital.

On each occasion, the sense of call has been critical to making the big decision to relocate and has also been a massive dynamo that has helped keep us going when things are tough.

Why is a sense of call so important?

- It gives a personal sense of confidence. Knowing that God has called you confirms that starting this church is one of the reasons God made you. It gives you a sense of destiny that propels you into the future with real energy and passion. You walk differently, talk differently and lead differently as a result of being called!

- It gives you faith for the growth of the church. Having been called by God you can approach the whole process knowing that God will give you success. This sense of faith will prove to be a powerful weapon as you learn to overcome the obstacles that will undoubtedly come across your path. It also communicates in many intangible but important ways to those who are thinking of joining you. It will help convince them that God is going to do something great and that they should join you to be a part of the action.

- It gives you faith that God will enable you to grow a new church. There will be times when you find yourself wondering whether God could have really called you to do this enormous task! In moments like this it is fortifying to remember that God will give you everything you need to accomplish it.

How does a call come?

A call can come in a number of different ways. These include:

1. A growing internal conviction

This is often connected with a sense that God is speaking to you in your personal times of prayer. This sense of personal certainty is the most important element in any call. You need to know God has called you. This sense often develops over time, although there can be key moments within that process of confirmation. If you are married it is also essential that your spouse shares this sense of conviction that God is calling you.

2. Clear supernatural experiences and/or prophetic words

'During the night Paul had a vision of a man of Macedonia standing and begging him, "Come over to Macedonia and help us." After Paul had seen the vision, we got ready at once to leave for Macedonia, concluding that God had called us to preach the gospel to them.'

Acts 16:9–10

Supernatural confirmations are wonderfully encouraging and God often provides these sorts of experiences for us.

'Before we decided to plant a church in Dublin we wanted to be sure that God was in this and we also wanted the children to feel a sense of calling too.

We did not say anything to the children, but continued to pray that God would speak to us. A few mornings later our daughter Anna described to us a dream she'd had in which we had moved house. The dream included lots of very specific details about the house that we moved to and included it's colour, a gravel drive, a sun dial in the garden and many other details.

Two days into our trip to Dublin Anna screamed as we passed an Estate Agent, "That is the house I saw in my dream!" We booked to see the house the next day and found every detail from Anna's dream, just as she had told us. It was a wonderful confirmation for us that we were pursuing God's plans and that there was great blessing ahead for us in Dublin.'

Chris and Rachel Vincent, Saoirse, Dublin

3. *The exhortation and direction of leaders in the church*

'News of this [salvation in Antioch] reached the ears of the church at Jerusalem, and they sent Barnabas to Antioch. When he arrived and saw the evidence of the grace of God, he was glad and encouraged them all to remain true to the Lord with all their hearts. He was a good man, full of the Holy Spirit and faith, and a great number of people were brought to the Lord. Then Barnabas went to Tarsus to look for Saul, and when he found him, he brought him to Antioch.'

Acts 11:22–26

Sometimes, those who know us well see gifts and abilities in us that we are unaware of. It is their encouragement and belief in us that causes us to ask whether God is speaking through them.

In my experience, this is one of the most common ways that God starts to give us a sense of being called. You cannot simply move on your leader's faith, you will need to hear God for yourself, but God sometimes uses other people's exhortations to get your attention.

David Coak had been successfully pastoring a church in Sussex for many years before he and Margaret started to sense that God was speaking to them about moving on to start all over again:

'We began to feel "disconnected" from the local scene, which was somewhat disconcerting. We wondered whether we were losing vision and interest!

It was around this time that we had a very powerful prophetic word from Terry Virgo about fresh challenges and these words sunk deep into our hearts. However, it was not clear where we should go.

Then one day I was in a leaders' meeting when Dave Holden made a brief comment that perhaps someone should church plant in Cambridge. Both Margaret and I felt an immediate response and assurance that that was where God wanted us to go, although neither of us had ever visited the city before!

That certainty gave us real strength when the inevitable challenging seasons came and helped us forge a church of 300 people before moving on again.'

David Coak, Emmanuel Church, Oxford

I have sometimes met people who know that God has spoken to them through their leaders and their own sense of conviction, but are waiting for something 'more supernatural'. If you fall into this category I want to encourage you to get going without delay. God speaks to us in different ways at different times. He knows what we need. One type of direction is no better than another. What is important is that we know in our own hearts what the Lord is saying. When we do, it is time for action.

'In 1996 I had a very vivid and totally unexpected dream in which I was leaving my church in Bedford and arriving somewhere to plant a church. I woke up my wife Louise there and then, in the middle of the night, and told her what I believed God had said. She asked where we were going, which seemed a reasonable question in the circumstances, but that was not at all clear at the time.

Over the next two years we became increasingly clear that we were to plant a church made up of people from many different cultures.

Then, as I was reading through Acts, I realised that it is as biblical to be sent to where there is a need (like Timothy, Titus and Philip) as it is to be called to a specific place. So, I went and spoke to David Stroud and David Devenish and offered to go wherever I could be useful.

After a certain amount of talking and praying we went to visit an inner city area in Birmingham. On our first visit there we saw many places I had seen several years before in my dream – even down to very specific, small details.

We concluded that God had spoken to us and in 1998 we started The Crown (taken from Isaiah 62: "No longer will they call your land desolate ... the nations will see your righteousness ... you will be a crown of splendour in the Lord's Hand") in the Handsworth area of Birmingham.'

Martin White, The Crown, Birmingham

4. It should always involve the affirmation of those who will oversee the church plant

The advice and care of leaders who will help us get the church planted will prove to be invaluable in due course, so make sure they are on board before you start. The last thing you want is to have made a move or got things started only to hear that these leaders felt 'jump started' into the whole process and were never quite sure whether God had called you to do this in the first place.

'I knew God was calling me to church leadership of some sort, having been a youth leader for a good few years. Some leaders were expressing doubt about whether I was ready. I realised that I was a church planter when sitting round a table with David and Philippa Stroud over a meal. David showed me a list of different styles of leadership and asked some pointed questions. As we talked, I realised that sorting out someone else's mess as a "re-engineering" leader would have killed me. The one that grabbed me was being an *"entrepreneurial" leader. Round that table, coffee in hand, I knew I was a pioneer and needed to plant churches. As we evaluated whether to take on a church that needed a leader or plant a new one – that was all I needed.'*

Andy Moyle, church planter in St Ives and King's Lynn

What do I do if I am not sure whether I am called?

If you are not sure whether God has called you then there are several things that you can do:

- Continue to serve in the church where you are currently based. Have a look at the list of skills that you should be developing in the next chapter and continue to work on these while you wait for God to give you further clarity.

- Ask your local church leadership and members of the apostolic team that they work with to tell you what they really think about you going to plant a church in the future. Listen carefully to their comments and any advice that they have for you.

- Continue to seek the Lord. Make this a subject of daily or weekly prayer until you are sure that he has spoken to you.

To become clear that God has called you to plant a church is a great start, but this is when the importance of preparation really kicks in.

You need to prepare yourself for what lies ahead and you do this by understanding how God prepares leaders to plant churches, and by working out what personal skills you need to develop. We will examine this more closely in the next section.

'As the Piper comes in at the Gates of Dawn, Rat turns to his friend Mole. "It's gone," sighed Rat. "So beautiful and strange and new! Since it was to end so soon, I almost wish I had never heard it. For it has roused a longing in me that is pain, and nothing seems worthwhile but just to hear that sound once more and go on listening to it forever. No! There it is again! Now it passes on and I begin to lose it," he said presently. "O Mole! The beauty of it! The merry bubble and joy, the thin, clear happy call of the distant piping! Such music I never dreamed of, and the call in it is stronger than even the music is sweet! Row on Mole, row! For the music and the call must be for us."'

The Wind in the Willows[1]

3

PREPARATION OF A
CHURCH PLANTER

'By failing to prepare, you are preparing to fail.'

Benjamin Franklin

'Leadership develops daily, not in a day.'[1]

John Maxwell

'For by the grace given me I say to every one of you: Do not think of yourself more highly than you ought, but rather think of yourself with sober judgment, in accordance with the measure of faith God has given you.'

Romans 12:3

'I [Paul] went immediately into the Arabia desert and later returned to Damascus. Then after three years, I went up to Jerusalem to get acquainted with Peter and stayed with him fifteen days.'

Galatians 1:17–18

As I look back, God used many different factors to prepare me to plant my first church. One of the most beneficial was the hours of time that I spent with David Devenish, who was my pastor at the time. I would often join David for his times of prayer, sit alongside him as he helped people who were struggling with life-controlling habits or spend time asking him questions about every aspect of Christian life and ministry. Leadership is more 'caught than taught' and I caught a lot from David during that time!

Later, I worked full time on the staff of Woodside Church in Bedford and took responsibility at different times for many areas of church life. By the time I was ready to plant a church I had already had hands-on experience at leading and overseeing most aspects of church life.

However, even more important for my preparation were the personal challenges that I faced during that period. Learning to be a good friend, a good husband and, in time, a good father; trusting God for resources that I did not have, coping under pressure and in times of conflict. It is the formation of us as people that is the most important part of the preparation of a leader and one that cannot be missed if we really want to be used by God.

What are the most important factors during times of preparation?

There are a number of things that typically happen during the preparation period before starting a church:

1. *We grow in our relationship with God*

'But Jesus often withdrew to lonely places and prayed.'

Luke 5:16

To lead God's people requires that we have a depth of relationship with him that enables us to lead people towards him.

Periods of preparation are wonderful opportunities to spend time with God in prayer and Bible study – to grow in our knowledge of him and to get to know him better and to learn to hear his voice more clearly. These periods might also include particular seasons of fasting and seeking God, allowing him to speak to us and shape us for future ministry.

2. *God shapes our character to be able to handle the challenges ahead.*

God's preparation is primarily focused on who we are becoming, not what we are doing. The best leaders minister out of *who they are,* not simply *what they know.* Therefore, God is always focused on the shaping of us as individuals.

'When Philippa and I got engaged I suggested we stayed in Bedford for another year. We then expected to move on to a larger city context.

However, God kept us where we were for almost ten more years. During that time we sometimes lived restlessly, treating the town we were living in as a "staging post". We did not really give ourselves to the people or the place in the way we should have.

Eventually, we understood how Jesus gave himself to those he lived amongst. We repented of our pride and told God we would be happy to stay for the rest of our lives. This was an important step for us and one that I'm sure God had been waiting for. Within a year, God was moving us on and we were preparing to move to the second largest city in the nation.'

David Stroud

God wants to teach us the importance of submitting every area of our lives to him. When you are being prepared by God, allow him to mould and shape you. He wants to make you a leader from the inside out!

3. *God develops and clarifies our calling*

As we serve God in different areas of church life we start to become clearer on who God has made us to be and what he has called us to do.

This requires us to be ready to look directly and honestly at our own strengths and weaknesses and receive feedback from others. This can be enormously helpful, for such feedback helps us to identify the areas in which we particularly need to grow and develop.

People who really understand what God has made them for often experience a deep sense of peace and ease about the roles that God gives them and this, in turn, makes them much more effective in whatever ministry God has called them to.

4. *We serve in the church*

This gives us a broad set of references that we can draw on in the future as the church planting process develops and we find ourselves reflecting back on lessons learned in the past regarding how to serve and lead in various areas of church life.

If we are planting a *Newfrontiers* church it is essential to have been part of another *Newfrontiers* church prior to this, so that we have first hand experience of what the implementation of those values looks like.

'After struggling as a Christian for years, I was prophesied over and then baptised in the Holy Spirit during a church meeting. Everything about my life, calling and future changed in those moments. I suddenly knew God wanted me to plant a church.

One of the elders started to disciple me and invited me to live in a shared house with him. Years of habitual sin and character weaknesses were confronted and dealt with. I learnt how to study, memorise scripture and express my leadership gift. I was then given opportunities to lead small groups and speak at the Alpha course.

Later, I was asked to come on staff and given responsibilities that felt far beyond my experience and maturity. The lead elder, Dave Stroud, guided me through each step and even invited me to live with his growing family in order to keep developing me 24/7! I was encouraged to complete my theological studies and learn to pastor people on the job.

Even though my wife and I wanted to go church planting, Dave asked me to lead the church when he sensed God directing him elsewhere. This huge jump into leadership forced me again to pursue spiritual renewal in my own life, taught me obedience and was perfect training for going planting myself four years later.'

Matt Hatch, Mosaic Church, Leeds

What skills do I need to develop when preparing to plant a church?

There are a number of skills and experiences that I would strongly recommend a potential church planter develops before being sent out:

1. Multiply small groups

So many of the skills that you will develop whilst leading a small group are key to church planting. You will learn a range of pastoral skills, including how to build community, care for the broken and stop needy people dominating a meeting. You will also have an opportunity to develop the key leadership skills of identifying, training and releasing leaders to start a new group.

You will use these abilities over and over again in your new setting. Don't leave home without having acquired them!

2. *Be involved in Alpha or other key evangelistic activities*

Any new church that is started must have mission at its heart, which means that you must have experience of connecting with those who do not know Jesus and helping them to find him.

Running an Alpha Course and a discussion group will sharpen your ability to communicate the gospel and share your story with different audiences. Importantly, it also gives you opportunities to challenge people to respond to the gospel and to lead them through the steps of repentance and faith.

3. *Lead a ministry and recruit, motivate and lead a team in that context*

During the church planting process you will often have to ask people to do a job in the church. You will also need to learn to keep them motivated once they are doing it.

To start the church planting process with these skills under your belt will be of enormous benefit.

4. *Speak in a mid-size group*

It will also be very beneficial if you have had some experience of speaking to groups of 30–75 people. This will help you get a good feel of what it will be like to preach to your new church and give you opportunities to hear feedback from others. Don't overlook hidden opportunities to craft a talk with the youth or children's work or during an Alpha course.

5. *Sit in on elders' or leadership team meetings*

This might not always be possible, but where available it will provide an enormous benefit in terms of learning how a church is led and the issues that are discussed (and not discussed) in elders' meetings. I still remember some of the insightful discussions I listened to and the wise decisions that I witnessed being made.

*   *   *

As God continues to shape and prepare you it is inevitable that you find yourself starting to think about where you might want to go to plant a church. This is a critical decision that can play a significant role in affecting how the church plant goes, so it is worth giving some time to. This is the subject of the next chapter.

4

HOW DO YOU DECIDE
WHERE TO GO?

'The LORD had said to Abram, "Leave your country, your people and your father's household and go to the land I will show you."'

Genesis 12:1

'A godly man in the wrong place will still produce only mediocre results.'[1]

Rick Warren

As Philippa and I began to consider whether we should move to London, we felt that the best thing to do was to actually spend a day praying and walking around in the Capital.

At this point in time we had not told anyone else about our plans, but as we were driving down the M40 towards London we received a prophetic word by text message! It read, 'You are like a plant that has outgrown its pot. It is time to be re-planted.'

We were absolutely staggered that God would speak to us in this way on the particular day that we had set aside to go down to London. It left us in little doubt that this was the right move for us.

We have been very fortunate on other occasions that the decision regarding where to plant has also been relatively straightforward. We had clear prophetic direction when we started our first church in Bedford and our move to Birmingham was precipitated by those we looked to for oversight asking us to go.

However, it is not always like that. Sometimes a leader knows that he should go, but doesn't know where to go.

This is an important decision. Our effectiveness will not be the same in every community. People are different in different places. We will connect with some better than others. Some communities are more open to the gospel than others.

We should be looking for God to speak through our minds, through our leaders and through supernatural guidance. By the time we are sure that God is speaking to us we have often experienced all three of these elements at work.

Remember that the decision often takes a little while and there are some important questions to ask along the way.

Is there a clear apostolic strategy that you are working to?

Paul the apostle had a clear strategy that we can see from the descriptions of his journeys in Acts.

He clearly prioritised the major cities in each area that he went to. Antioch, Thessalonica, Corinth, Philippi, Athens, Ephesus and Rome were all regional capitals. Once Paul had started churches in these areas he was able to say that he had, 'no more place for me to work in these regions' (Rom. 15:23).

In other words, Paul did not complete the whole mission himself. Rather, he started churches in key centres and then looked to other church planters to start other churches in the surrounding areas.

Effectively, Paul broke the area open and then looked for others to fill in with churches all around. The church planters who started these churches would have been fulfilling the apostolic strategy that was in Paul's heart.

As you start to pray and seek God regarding where you should plant a church, I would encourage you to talk with the apostolic team that you are working with and make sure you are clear what their current strategy is and how you can contribute towards it.

'A few years after planting my first church, God spoke to David Devenish about planting and establishing fifty churches in the Midlands over a five-year period. Our move to Birmingham to plant a new church was to assist in fulfilling the apostolic strategy that David had laid out.

This made a massive difference to how we felt: we knew we were playing our part in reaching a whole region with the gospel. Rather than simply working by ourselves tucked away in a big city with little hope of having any worthwhile impact, we were ministering in tandem with others and trusting that along with them we could make a genuine difference.'

David Stroud

God's direction

Paul seemed to combine a sense of overall strategic direction whilst looking for God's immediate direction for the next step.

We are told he was *'kept by the Holy Spirit from preaching the word … in Asia'* and that *'the Spirit of Jesus'* would not allow them to enter Bithynia. But then God gave him a dream in the night and the next day they were on their way to modern day Greece (Acts 16:6–10).

We will do well to combine these two elements: over-arching apostolic strategy and more immediate Spirit-led direction.

If we want to have a genuine impact on this nation then we cannot ignore the strategic priorities of its big cities. However, it would be foolish to simply pursue the 'strategic' course without looking for God's specific direction. Sometimes he will surprise us as we gain a sense of what he is saying to us. His knowledge of the future, of our potential and limitations, means he makes the perfect call on where we should be every time.

What sort of church plant should you embark upon?

There are at least two different types of church plant that we can be involved with:

1. *A church plant close to an existing church*

In this model a church sends a significant team from the existing congregation to start a new church (often 20–50 people) within easy travelling distance.

It may begin with a small group being started in the area with the members of that group returning to the existing church for Sunday worship and other church activities.

There are many advantages to planting churches this way.

- The church planting team can continue to draw on the benefits of a stronger, established church nearby. This massively reduces the sense of isolation that a team can feel in the early days of starting a new church.

- It reduces the need for people to move home. It may well be that some of the team are already living in

the area that the new church is focused on. This
means there is less need to move, find new jobs or
new schools.

- There is often a much higher level of support for the
new leaders because there are other churches and
members of the apostolic team reasonably close by.

- There are sometimes relationships with unbelievers
that have already been formed by members of the
church planting team and others in the community.
This gives the team a valuable sense of momentum
as it often takes a while to get to know people well in
a new setting.

2. A long range church plant

This takes place at a greater distance from the existing
congregation and therefore typically involves a smaller
team (5–20 people) who have to find new jobs, buy new
homes and find new schools for their children.

This sort of church planting can open up whole new
areas or cities to the gospel. It has a higher level of risk
than the first type, but it also has a much greater potential
for the onward progress of the gospel and multiple other
church planting opportunities.

This sort of 'parachute' church planting is normally
most suited to those who have some experience of church
planting already and are prepared to put themselves
into an even more challenging environment for further
pioneering.

This type of long distance church plant will often
draw together a diverse team from different parts of the
country, rather than simply from one or two churches in
a distinct locality.

Long distance church plants are recorded in Acts 8:4–40
and Acts 11:19–21, although on both these occasions it

seems to have been persecution that catalysed the moving process!

What sort of area should I plant a church in?

Not every area is the same and it is therefore important to consider the different characteristics of church planting in different settings:

1. *Large cities*

It was these sorts of cities that were at the centre of Paul's focus on his church planting journeys.

City church planting has a number of other advantages:

- *It enables us to reach many people.* Cities, of course, are where the most people dwell – over 50% of the world's population now live in the city.

- *It enables us to reach key people who live in the centre of the city.* We must remember that whilst people will come in from the suburbs to the heart of the city, the people in the centre of the city will not come out to the suburbs to church. Consequently, we must plant churches in the centre of our cities if we are going to reach the key opinion formers and cultural shapers of society.

- *It enables us to influence wider culture.* We must bear in mind that 'as the city goes, so goes the culture'. In other words, the people who dwell in the city have a disproportionate effect on the shaping of culture. If Christians are to take seriously the mandate to be 'salt and light' (Matt. 5:13–16), then it is important that we are planting churches in cities.

'When Stu came home one day and told me he thought we should move to London to plant a church, I was absolutely staggered. I had no desire to move back to London and was not excited about church planting. The last thing I wanted to do was to be relocating with any kind of reluctance or fear, so God had some work to do in my heart!

Over the next few months I spent time really seeking God for confirmation that this was what he wanted for us. Then, one night at a summer conference, God spoke to me as people prayed with me. I saw really clearly that if God had called Stu to go to Greenwich, then he had called me and he had called the whole family. Everything fell into place. From that moment on I was ready to go, we had a church to get started!'

Livy Gibbs, Emmanuel Church, Greenwich

2. Suburban and provincial towns

Suburban church planting has been relatively effective in the last couple of decades.

Suburbia is a welcoming environment for families and it is therefore a natural place for church planters to move with their families and then find other families to reach out to, as well as many other couples and single people.

3. Rural

It is important to be aware that there are often two communities living alongside each other in rural contexts. There are those who have lived in the area for generations and then the recent incomers.

The recent incomers tend to be more open to the gospel initially, but as churches become more involved in the community, in social action in particular, inroads can be made into the more traditional local community.

'*Rural communities are often small and spread out and therefore it is really important to locate our church plants strategically, so that we can reach the most people with the limited resources we have.*

We are constantly listening for God's direction, but we also look for other common sense pointers that a community might be ripe for church planting. These include the existence of a secondary school or a big supermarket – sure signs that this is a "hub community" which people will travel into for schooling and shopping and, we trust, church as well.'

**Dave Harper, Church in the Peak, Matlock,
Buxton and Chesterfield**

Where can I be the most effective?

There should be a 'fit' between the church planter and the community that God calls them to reach. Answering the questions below will help you assess the sort of community that will be a 'fit' for you:

1. Has God given you a burden for a particular people group or geographical area?

Sometimes it feels as though God gives us an element of choice in these things. If you do not have clear leading from the Lord then do not be afraid to simply ask yourself, 'Where would I like to go?'

Sometimes it is God's way of guiding us – he puts a passion for certain communities on our heart in order that they will be reached with the gospel.

2. Will you 'fit' in the area or with the people?

Will you make friends there easily? How will your spouse feel? Will you be happy living there? What will your children do about schooling? Are you happy with this?

Most people are most effective within the culture they identify most closely with. It is these people that they most naturally relate to, build friendships with and can reach out to.

Sometimes God will lead you beyond your own culture to another group of people, but if he does not, then reach out to those you most easily connect to.

3. *Have you been to the area?*

How did you feel walking the streets, going into the shops, talking to people who live there?

4. *Is this the sort of place that you can get a job if you need one?*

5. *What are the regional or apostolic team that you are working with saying?*

Do they have somewhere in mind? Is there an existing opportunity with a core team waiting for a leader to develop the church plant?

6. *How far is this from where you are currently living?*

How far is it from those who will oversee you? Bear in mind that the further away you are from the apostolic team who will be helping you plant the church, the less you are likely to see them.

Will the support that you need be available if you start a church here?

'We felt that it was time for us to get involved in church planting, but we did not have a clear sense of where God wanted us to go.

We knew that we wanted to go somewhere that was a centre of influence – not just a city in itself, but a city that could touch a region. We were looking for a place that could feed a pipeline of people that we could train and send out to plant churches all over the place, but apart from that we were not clear.

Then in the car going up to Leeds, my wife Pip, who has a strong prophetic gift, turned to me and said, "Matt, this is going to be it." As we got into the city and started to look around we felt a strong sense of faith that we were to do something in Leeds that would touch the ends of the earth.'

Matt and Pip Hatch, Mosaic Church, Leeds

Where in the town or city should I locate the church?

Once one has identified the town or city to move to, another question is raised: where in the town or city should you live and where should you plan to locate the church in due course?

'On some occasions I have had an instinctive sense of where I should start the church. This was the case in both Bedford and London. They were places that I knew well before I started church planting. I felt connected to the people, understood how people moved around and knew that in both cases a central location would work best for what God was asking me to do.

However, when I started in Birmingham it was different. I did not know the city at all. Consequently, I needed to spend a lot more time driving around, talking to people who lived there and seeking God to determine where in the city we should be located. It was not until I had been living in the city for some months that I felt that I had begun to understand it and the people who lived there.'

David Stroud

Here are some things to consider:

1. *As you get to know the area ask lots of questions,*
   such as ...

   - What sort of people live in each area?

   - How do people travel and move around the city?

   - Does everyone travel by car? How much do people
     use public transport? Does public transport run
     properly on Sundays?

   - Is this town/city made up of a number of smaller
     local identities and, if so, will people travel beyond
     these areas to come to church?

2. *Are there any similar churches in town to the one*
   that I am going to plant?

If so, where are they located? (see Chapter 22 which
contains a section on building relationships with other
churches).

3. *How far afield should I expect to draw people from?*

There are two mistakes that are often made in this
context:

   - Some people go for too small an area. This will
     mean that it will often take longer to get the church
     going, simply because there are fewer people in
     your mission field and therefore fewer are likely
     to come to Christ in any given year. Momentum is
     key to church planting (see Chapter 18: *Developing*
     Momentum) and it can be very hard to keep people
     with you if the start is very slow. In this situation
     you should consider broadening the area and
     number of people you are reaching out to.

   - Some people go for too large an area without the
     gifting or stature to carry it off. This results in

a small church that is dwarfed by the size of its mission field. Some newcomers will realise there is a mismatch between the leader's gifts and the size of the vision and will not stay as a result. This is where a church planting coach can be so helpful. As you are considering where to plant, ask for their input to help ensure there is a good 'match' between your gifts and the size of the area that you are seeking to reach out to.

Things to be doing whilst you are waiting for God to speak

1. *Keep praying*

This is an important decision and one that God will want to speak to you about. Be diligent and soak the whole process in prayer.

2. *Read*

Keep reading the Scriptures and books on planting churches. God will often speak to us unexpectedly as we are relaxed, have an enquiring heart and are open to him.

3. *Talk with the apostolic team*

Talk with those who will be sending you and others who know you well about what they see as God's next step for you and where you would be best suited.

As the location starts to become clear, so your vision for the church can start to grow. It becomes easier to imagine what the church will look like and what sort of people you will be ministering to as you can see the church in a particular location.

* * *

As the vision develops it should become a powerful tool in your hands to help you lead the church forward. The next section looks at how you do this in more depth. It will also help you to clarify the sort of church that God is calling you to build and show you how to share this with maximum effect.

5

DEVELOPING A VISION

'The LORD had said to Abram, "Leave your country, your people and your father's household and go to the land I will show you. I will make you into a great nation and I will bless you; I will make your name great, and you will be a blessing. I will bless those who bless you, and whoever curses you I will curse; and all peoples on earth will be blessed through you."'

Genesis 12:1–3

'*Foresight is the "lead" that the leader has. Once leaders lose this lead and events start to force their hand, they are leaders in name only. They are not leading; they are reacting to immediate events and they probably will not long be leaders.*'[1]

Robert Greenleaf

'*Champions aren't made in gyms. Champions are made from something they have deep inside them – a desire, a dream, a vision.*'

Muhammad Ali

I had no idea that the next words I would say would have such a powerful impact ... I was in a car with David

Devenish during the autumn of 1995, sharing with him what I felt the Lord had been saying to me about my next phase of ministry.

'I feel God is saying to me that it is "for Middle England",' I told him.

As I spoke these words, I could literally feel the Holy Spirit sweep into the car and I saw and heard the impact as David doubled over (in the passenger seat, thankfully!) and shouted out, 'That's what God has been saying to me!' This was not what I was expecting from a drive around the M25!

Whilst the presence of God filled the car, David went on to explain that whilst he was on holiday God had spoken to him and told him to start and establish fifty churches in the Midlands in the next five years.

David then found, to his amazement, that on his return to the UK he was contacted by a number of churches in the Midlands asking him for help.

Neither of us had been expecting God to speak to us so clearly, but the result of that journey was that we both knew that we had a new God-given vision to pursue.

For both of us, this vision to see fifty churches planted and established across the Midlands by the year 2000, shaped the next season of our lives and ministries. David drove literally thousands of miles to counsel leaders, appoint elders and encourage and strengthen churches. I uprooted my family from Bedford and moved to Birmingham to plant a new church there and also travelled many miles to bring about what we believed God had already planned.

A clear vision is a compelling picture of a God-given future. It does not often come in as dramatic fashion as David and I experienced on that occasion, but it is absolutely essential for any church planter to have a clear picture of what the church will look like before he begins.

The benefits of a vision

1. *It releases passion, energy, sacrifice and excitement*

It is a picture of the future that is worth giving your all for. It helps you get out of bed in the morning and it elicits high levels of motivation from others who are part of the team.

2. *It gives you a 'map' that enables many decisions to be made quickly*

As you clarify the sort of church that God is leading you to create, many decisions become much more straight-forward as a result. Apparently exciting opportunities can be judged on whether they will take you closer to your destination or whether they will actually prove to be a distraction for you in the end.

3. *It helps those who join the church plant early on to make a decision as to whether this is a church they want to be involved in building*

Because they now know what the church is going to become.

Every church planter must be ready to answer the question, 'What is your vision?' or 'What is this church going to be like?' This is important. You need to be able to paint a clear picture of the future, because the small group in your living room have no other way of seeing what God's future for them may hold.

Characteristics of a vision

1. *It is clear*

A vision should create a clear picture of God's intended future for the church.

It makes clear the size of the church, the area from which you are likely to draw people, the sorts of ministries that it will develop and the way in which it will reach out to others. It will express clearly the church's approach to church planting and mission and how it reaches out and cares for those who are part of the church and wider community.

2. It is God-honouring

Your vision will show clearly how the church and its activities will bring glory to God. The more clearly you can show that God will be glorified through the church, the more powerful your vision will be.

3. It is future orientated

A vision does not need to have a timescale attached to it (the Midlands initiative that I spoke about at the start of this section was unusual in that regard), but it is focused on the future not the present.

4. It is compelling

As people listen to your vision they feel in their hearts that this 'must' be done. They find themselves wanting to lay aside other things so that they can prioritise building the church with you.

5. It provokes a clear sense of faith

A vision should always stretch people beyond what they think they can achieve to something that only God can achieve. A God-given vision always requires great faith.

> 'Attempt something so impossible that unless God is in it, it's doomed to failure.'
>
> John Haggai

6. *It provokes commitment*

Everybody needs a reason to live. A vision of God's purposes, worked out through the local church, will provide this for each person who is involved. It is amazing to see the levels of sacrifice that people are prepared to make for a vision that clearly has the hand of God upon it.

7. *It shows what your particular church is going to be like, as opposed to every other church*

Whilst the New Testament provides us with clear principles on which every local church should be built, each local church should also express something of the uniqueness of God's creation in the 'personality' that it develops.

It is important to think through what sort of people are likely to join the church (who lives in the area that you are going to meet in? Who are you most able to connect with and draw into the church?) and therefore what style of worship music is appropriate. How long should the preaching be? What style of small group ministry is most appropriate? etc.

'What an eventful first drive from London to Manchester I had, with Steve Nicholson's words ringing out of my car's cassette player. It was 1993.

"The trouble with many leaders is that they have lost the will to dream big dreams. What are your big dreams?" Steve asked.

My reply, instinctively and audibly back to the cassette recorder was, "I want to plant twenty churches in Greater Manchester."

This moment was the start of a journey.

Beginning with a very small core group we were captivated by that seemingly impossible challenge.

We developed a strategy that broke the normal rules of building a large resource church and then planting out. In the first year, as *we gathered our first fifty people, we also started two new churches. More church plants followed as we took risks and reached out across the North West of England. Faith was high and a "have a go" culture permeated the people as they served and celebrated one another's successes. Owning a big vision caused all of us to over achieve!*

Last year we began building our sixth church in Greater Manchester, this time in the under-churched and poorer east side, and again we emphasized this bigger vision. Small mindedness and self-interest is a curse and we are always looking to lift people's horizons, to have a concern for the whole of Greater Manchester, this nation and the nations of the world.'

Colin Baron, Christchurch Manchester

How do you develop vision?

I contracted pneumonia shortly after starting to prepare to plant the King's Arms. This was very frustrating. I was excited about the church plant and could not wait to get going, but found myself having to put my plans on hold whilst I slowly recovered.

However, it proved to be very beneficial in one important way. During the weeks of recuperation I was able to work on articulating the vision that God had given me for the church. This took a lot longer than I had anticipated and required multiple drafts before I was anywhere near happy with it. Each draft felt a little like taking a layer off an onion. Each time I was closer to the core, but still had more work to do.

On other occasions when preparing to plant a church I have kept a document on the desktop of my computer and added things to it whenever I felt God speaking to me or simply had a thought that seemed insightful or inspirational. Later I would spend time praying over the disparate thoughts I had jotted down and attempt to synthesise them into a more coherent sense of vision.

The development of vision has always taken longer and proven to be harder work than I anticipated. Even when there are moments of great revelation, the impact of these tends to take some time to work out and apply in the situation I'm in.

However, the hard work has always been worth it. Clarity is a very powerful thing in the hands of a leader. This process is an essential part of the leader getting clear on what God is calling them to do.

Here are some steps that will assist you as you seek to articulate the vision that God has put in your heart:

1. Read the Scriptures

As you read you are checking your own heart to ensure that you embrace and value every principle outlined in Scripture, ensuring that these will be reflected clearly in your vision. These biblical principles should become powerful foundations in the life of the church. (See *Appendix A: What Sort of Church Are We Trying to Build? – Principles for New Testament Church Life*).

2. Pray and seek God

Very often God speaks to a leader on his knees. Make sure that you soak the whole process of developing vision in prayer as you are going along.

3. Be open to God speaking to your own heart through prophetic direction and other supernatural experiences

The way in which God sometimes 'apprehends' us can be tremendously helpful as your vision is starting to take shape. For me, prophetic words that have come in the preparatory phase of a church plant have often helped me believe God for more than I would have done otherwise.

4. *Draw out what God has already put in your heart*

Over the years God puts passion in our hearts and gives us particular burdens which stay with us. An important part of developing vision is to identify these and articulate them. Sometimes asking yourself questions can help you in this. Use questions like:

- What do I want the church to look like in ten years time ... in twenty years time?
- What do I want the church to look like when I hand over the leadership to someone else?
- What sort of church would I build if God made all the resources available to me that I ever needed, including anointing, fellow leaders, buildings and money?
- Is the vision clear? Is it challenging and does it inspire people to action?

5. *Draw on other references*

As you develop vision you will find that you are drawing consciously and unconsciously on other churches that you have read about or visited. It is good to draw on these influences, but ensure that the principles you learn from them are properly integrated with the values you hold dear and are applied well into your context. Beware of simply bolting onto your vision the latest exciting thing that is happening in the Christian world.

6. *Remember, your vision is shaped by your context*

The context into which you are ministering has a significant effect on the way in which you shape the church.

Ministry in a rural area and ministry in a large urban centre require very different approaches. You need to articulate your vision in such a way that it fits the particular area you are working in.

7. *Share your developing vision with those overseeing the church for input and comment*

Take the opportunity to discuss your developing vision with your coach. It is invariably helpful to be able to express this to others and to receive their feedback, especially from those who have experience in developing and casting vision themselves. (See also *Appendix B: Mission, Vision and Values Worksheet*.)

> 'Vision is something that you discover. You are discovering what God has put inside of you. You are looking for his plans.'

'I spent a number of months of really deep soul searching and interaction with God to work out what was really in my heart, what was my passion. I realised it wasn't just to have a big church or to be successful. Deep down I knew that wasn't enough.

What I was after was a church that saw people coming to Christ on a very regular basis. I had to build the sort of church where the longer you were in it, the more non-Christian friends you would develop, not less as is normally the case.

Once I was clear on that, my next challenge was to work out how to create a church with this burden at its centre ...'

Tony Thompson, Hope Church, Luton

Casting a vision

When asked how he spent his spare time, Churchill answered, 'Preparing off the cuff speeches.'

Casting vision can have an electrifying effect upon a church plant. It lifts heads that are down, inspires those who are already committed and draws in those who are looking to make their contribution in a place where God is going to be glorified.

However, church planters rarely share their vision often enough. They forget that some of the people were not present the last time they shared it, that new people have arrived who need to hear it, and that it does the regular members a lot of good to hear it all again.

'Share your vision often enough so that those who are part of your core are mouthing the words along with you!'

Steve Nicholson
Leader, Vineyard Church Planting task force, USA

---

1. *You need to have your vision ready to present in three different formats:*

- **30 seconds.** This is for the, 'So, why are you starting a new church?' type of question that you will get from your neighbours and others you meet when you explain, 'I have just moved into the town.'

- **3 minutes.** This is for the more interested person at the end of a small group meeting or at a gathering event.

- **30 minutes.** This is for when you are preaching.

Do not assume that clear, articulate vision simply flows when you are asked for it. Rather, take the time to prepare these different versions of your vision. It will not only prepare you for the opportunities to come, but is a great test of how clear you are on what God has given you to do.

'The first time I cast a three minute vision was to other Christians who were wondering about joining a church planting team. I had not prepared as carefully as I should and the leader after me spoke more succinctly and with more clarity than I had. As a result, he got a lot more interest from people.

That was a hard lesson learned. Since then, I have worked much harder at preparing the thirty second and three minute visions and sharing them with as many people as I can.'

Andy Moyle, The Gateway Church, King's Lynn

2. Stories are a great way of encapsulating key parts of your vision

Look for any stories from your own life and experience, as well as from others, that sum up different aspects of your vision. These stories can become very powerful culture formers. You should repeat them often.

3. Make sure that you are inspired and motivated by your vision

If you are not, then others won't be either!

4. In the early phases of the church plant, look for every opportunity you can to informally share your vision or an aspect of it

You can do this over a cup of coffee, at the start of a small group meeting or over a meal.

5. As the church develops look for regular opportunities when you can share your vision with the whole church

Church anniversaries, the start of the term or the beginning of the year are all good times to do this.

6. Meetings particularly geared towards new members are a great place in which to share your vision

There is no better way of drawing people into the church than sharing with them where you believe God is taking the church over the next season.

*   *   *

As you become equipped with a clear, compelling vision of what you believe God wants to do, you are in a very strong place to start to recruit a team. Sharing this vision will be a powerful tool in drawing others to join you. The next section looks at the process of recruiting a team in some detail.

6

RECRUITING A CHURCH PLANTING TEAM

Recruiting the church planting team often feels like the start of the adventure.

Before we told the church in Bedford that we were moving to Birmingham, we spoke with key leaders and friends to share with them personally what we believed we should do.

One of the couples we sat down with were our good friends, Adrian and Lucy Hurst. At the time, Adrian was working full time for the church I was leading in Bedford and Lucy was in the middle year of her degree.

As we shared with them that we were planning on leaving Bedford to plant a new church they told us they wanted to come too. We were thrilled that they wanted to come, but explained that the church plant had no money with which to pay Adrian. With Lucy being in the middle of a demanding degree we knew that meant that there would be very little opportunity for either of them to get a paying job. We could not see a way in which their idea was going to work out.

To our surprise, however, they came back to us a few days later and told us, 'We want to come anyway. We believe that we should live by faith, trusting God for our income.'

We were bowled over by the amazing courage and faith that this demonstrated.

By the end of the year they had received more income 'living by faith' than in the previous year when Adrian had been employed!

As I look back, I also have no idea how we would have got the church started in Birmingham without Adrian's help.

Why do you need a church planting team?

Finding the first ten people is the hardest part of starting a church. After that, the greatest challenge is getting the first twenty and then the first fifty.

This is why I would always encourage church planters to gather a team before they start planting a church. If you can gather a team of ten you will never have to do the hardest part of planting a church. If you can gather a team of twenty then you have just crossed the second hardest hurdle and you may not even have had your first church plant meeting.

What is a 'church planting team'?

A church planting team is the initial group that you gather prior to moving or starting the actual church plant.

This can be as small as simply you and your family (despite what I have said about the benefits of a good sized group, some people plant successfully with just their immediate family as the initial team) or as large as fifty or more people.

The size of the team and the various gifts that you are looking for depend on where and how you plan to start the church.

Identifying your needs

To my mind there are two types of people that make up any church planting team:

- First, there are people who you need to fulfil key roles. What these roles are will be determined by your own strengths and weaknesses.

- Second, there are other workers – good hearted, able individuals who understand what you are trying to do and want to support the vision. They may, in time, also become leaders in the church as well.

Here are the key issues you should consider as you begin to focus on assembling your church planting team:

1. *What are your key strengths and gifts and what roles do you need to be filled by the team?*

Make sure you think through your own strengths and weaknesses and then find people to join your team who will complement your strengths and bolster your weaknesses.

At the start of a church plant you may have to do many things for which you do not feel gifted, but nevertheless have to be done. However, if you can find a few others to fill specialist roles, then that will save you a lot of hard work and precious time that could be spent on other things more suited to your own gifts and abilities.

'From the outset we felt that God had spoken to us about gathering fifty committed adults and to expect 100 at the launch. So we set a date in the diary and prayed and worked our way towards these targets. Each enquiry was valued and followed up by a personal meeting; we prayed in the team one by one and were quite specific with our prayers. At one point, I remember very clearly being on my knees in my study praying, "Lord, we need a bass player"!'

Chris Kilby, Life Southampton

2. *What launch strategy are you going to pursue?*

The launch strategy is fully discussed in Chapter 16. You may want to have a glance at that chapter whilst you are working through this chapter.

If you are going to start a Sunday morning meeting very quickly after beginning the church plant, then you need to ensure that you have certain key players:

- *At least one good musician* who plays either the guitar or keyboard and ideally is someone who can actually lead the new church in worship. If you start with a reasonable quality of music then you will attract other musicians. Musicians typically settle in churches where there is already a good standard of music, so recruiting one or two quality musicians early on is a good strategy.

- *A capable leader with a heart for children's work.* Ideally, you are looking for someone who can coordinate a number of different age groups, set the standard for what you are trying to do and think through issues regarding security, recruiting others and so on.

In most UK contexts many people who will join your church are likely to be young families. This means that the quality of your children's work is a big issue. If the children want to return the following week there is a good chance that their parents will do so! However, if the children don't enjoy what you are doing, even after repeated visits, then the parents are much more likely to look elsewhere.

- *Several experienced small group leaders.* This will help you go to multiple small groups early on. Otherwise, you will have to wait whilst you train people from scratch. Having experienced leaders has the added benefit of providing you with more people who are friendly and ready to reach out to others and they are very valuable, whether it is for welcoming people on a Sunday, providing pastoral support as the church begins to grow or bringing new people into their cells.

- You may find there are some people available who are not leaders but who are *good at inviting others to events.* They help set a culture early on and can be invaluable members of the team.

- You also need *other able bodied individuals who will help where needed.* This will tend to be in the setting up and packing down of Sunday meetings, and they will also assist in providing some level of critical mass on Sundays, contribute during the worship, start to give financially, etc.

'We were going to be moving fifty miles to plant in King's Lynn. We knew no one there and we would need to somehow hit the ground running. I felt we could gather more quickly to a public meeting than small groups, partly because of my gift mix and largely because we had the finances to make a big splash. I needed a good sized core team to do that.

I drew up a wish list of people – a musician, small group leaders, someone in their twenties to gather other twenty somethings and work with the youth, a children's worker and a drummer!

I also wanted to start with a leadership team. I had a few names I wanted to headhunt. Andy and Jenny were first on the list and would fill the roles of musician, small group leader and part of my leadership team. I grabbed them one Sunday to arrange a coffee. "You're not asking us to go planting with you to King's Lynn are you?" they asked. This was even before it was public news. "Err, yes," I replied. It was not how I had planned the conversation would go, but within a fortnight the shock had died down and they were on board.

Jason had told me that whenever I planted again he would come, so he said yes straight away. Laura had been our first convert as youth leaders and was now living in Leeds. One Sunday night I called her to discover she was skiving church that evening to seek God for her future. "You should come to King's Lynn, lead the youth and gather 20s," I suggested. She was on board within days and gave me the number of another family who were moving to the area as well.

All but one of our core team came because I asked them, so I learned the importance of being proactive in asking and not relying on media like the Internet and print to gather people. Conventional planting wisdom says that students, 20s and retirees are the most likely people to get involved, but God gave us a much broader team than that. He also worked in his providence so that I asked people at just the right time.'

Andy Moyle, Gateway Church, King's Lynn

3. *Look for people with good character*

In the early days of bringing a team together you can sometimes feel so desperate to draw people in that you find yourself considering those you would otherwise pass by – often because they have ongoing pastoral issues. You should be very wary of doing this as such people are likely to be a significant drain on your time. Remember that the issues a person has do not disappear by them moving town to join a new church plant. In fact, in a smaller setting where you are trusting God for breakthrough, such issues often get magnified.

It is better to ask someone *not* to join the team than to find that they are a major drain on your time and leadership once you are starting the church. It is much better to stay focused on recruiting those who you know will have enough energy to contribute to what you are doing.

Conversely, reliable, faithful men and women who are ready to look beyond themselves and serve God and other people through countless hours of hosting new people, setting up and packing down on a Sunday and giving financially are priceless to any church plant.

4. *Do not overestimate the change that men and women will make in moving to a new venture*

Sometimes when people need a new challenge they can 'come alive' in a new setting and a church plant can provide 'room' for individuals to grow in ways that were not possible in their previous church. However, most of the time people do not change significantly simply by making a move.

'I have not always been as careful as I should have been about recruiting members for my church planting teams. As a result there have been times, early in the church plant, when I have found myself mediating between two members who have fallen out or wondering whether I will have to initiate church discipline because someone who came to plant a church has been indulging in inappropriate sexual behaviour instead!

If you think an individual is not ready to join you, then it is kindest to them, the rest of the team, and those you are trying to reach, for you to be honest enough to tell them.'

Anonymous

How do you go about recruiting people for the team?

1. *Pray and ask God to bring people to you*

Every step of the church planting process should be soaked in prayer and the gathering of a team is no exception. God often answers these prayers in remarkable ways.

'When we moved to London to start ChristChurch London there were a number of friends of ours who were living in different parts of the country who we contacted to ask whether they would think and pray about joining us.

One particular instance stands out in my mind. This is what Paul said: "If you had asked me during any other week of my life I would have said, 'We cannot come with you because we cannot afford to buy a home in London.' However, my mother died last week and left me a significant inheritance. This means that, for the first time in my life, we could afford to do it. We will pray and see what God says!"

We left praising God for his faithfulness. If we had asked on any other occasion, they would have turned us down immediately. However, God clearly had other plans. In due course, Paul and Anne came back to us and said they felt God was saying they should join us.

However, the story did not end there. Subsequently our friends put their house on the market but had great trouble selling it.

We happened to be visiting members of our family who lived close to them, so we decided to drive past their house and see whether there was a 'sold' board up yet. The sign outside told us there had been no interested parties, but Philippa spoke out a prayer: "Lord, please sell Paul and Anne's house quickly now." We all said, "Amen!"

Paul and Anne called the very next week to say they'd had a viewer around the next day who had made an offer on the house which they had accepted. The house was sold and they were moving to join the church planting team!'

David Stroud

2. *Talk to individuals and ask them to come with you*

Nothing beats a personal, face-to-face invitation to join the team. Wherever possible, I would avoid making this sort of 'ask' by phone or email. Instead, sit down with the person, look them in the eye and tell them why you would love them to come.

Most of the time people will need time to consider such a big proposition, especially when it involves moving house or changing job. This is very understandable. However, whilst they are deliberating, I will try and meet with them once or twice. It is much easier to comment and advise while people are making up their minds, rather than trying to offer a different perspective once people have made their decision.

3. *Let as many people as possible within your network know you are starting a new church*

Think of as many different ways as possible of getting the news out that a new church plant is starting. Websites, online videos and regular prayer and news emails all play their part in this.

Talk to your coach about other ways of sharing the news of your church plant more broadly. See if there are opportunities to share at regional celebrations or to preach at other churches on Sundays. Ask other church leaders whether they will promote your project and whether they would consider allowing some of their church members to join you.

4. Put on a day when people can come and meet you, hear about your vision and discuss the practical details of making a move

Don't make this a high pressure time, but rather a relaxed opportunity to build relationships with people and help them discover whether God is asking them to join you. Always make sure that it involves a meal together. Sharing food together is one of the best ways to bond with others, hear where they are at and give an opportunity for more personal questions and discussion.

5. There are several groups of people who are most likely to make a move:

- People who you already know and who have confidence in your leadership.

- People who are looking for a new challenge. Sometimes, people cannot find an obvious next step for their own growth in an established church setting. This is particularly the case in a larger church. You may need the assistance of your coach or the apostolic team you relate to, to meet or contact people in these churches, but they can often prove to be a fruitful place for finding potential team members.

- People who have a particular heart for the place where you are going to start the church or are particularly passionate about the type of people you are going to be reaching there.

6. Involve the leaders of the church in this process

Remember to involve the elders of churches in the process of inviting people to join you. This is particularly important if you are inviting people to join you from the church you are currently a part of. The leaders may have some good reasons for not wanting you to approach certain people or helpful suggestions on how to start such conversations.

Making the big ask

The most important moment in getting anyone to join you is when you sit down with them and ask them face to face. Here are a few pointers to bear in mind as you do that:

1. *Share your vision with people.* People will want to know what you are planning, what you are hoping to achieve and what it is going to look like. It is essential to share your hopes and dreams of what God might do.

2. *Build relationships with people.* Typically people want to know that you care before they follow you. In other words, before you influence people's minds you have to win their hearts. Building a good relationship with those people you are planning to ask is therefore a critical part of the process.

3. *Tell the individual or couple why you are specifically asking them.* Make the request personal. Explain why you are sitting down with this individual or couple, what it is that they would contribute and what a difference it would make to the new church plant if they were to join you.

4. *Ask people to pray about whether they should go before they ask themselves whether it is practically possible.* If it is God's will for them to join you then he can be trusted to overcome any obstacles that they are facing.

'I learned an important lesson in gathering a team when I asked some good friends of ours, Tim and Jacqui, to come with us to London.

They were eager to join us, having felt God speaking to them, but they did not know how they would manage it. Tim had just finished university and Jacqui had graduated the year before. They were just starting to pay off their student loans and did not have a significant income with which to rent a flat in central London.

Jacqui was working for a small advertising agency in Redhill, but out of the blue she received a call from one of the big advertising agencies in central London, asking her whether she would come and have a chat with them about a vacancy they wanted to fill.

The next day Jacqui went up to their London offices and spent thirty minutes talking with them. During that time she was told all about the job and the opportunities it would offer. Then the executive said to Jacqui, "There is just one question I have for you: how much would we need to pay you for you to make the move and come and join us?"

God had just opened the door for our good friends to make the move and join the church planting team!'

David Stroud

5. *Do not be put off by people who say 'no'.* Not everyone you ask will be able to come or even want to come. Don't be put off by those who say 'no'. Just make sure that you ask enough people in order to receive a sufficient number of 'yes's'.

Potential pitfalls

1. *Be careful about those who are looking for a leadership role because they cannot get one in their existing church*

If people you are talking to, or who approach you, are frustrated in their current setting, be careful before encouraging them to join you. A new start always looks attractive to frustrated individuals, but you should be sure that the frustrations they are currently struggling with are not more of a reflection of their own character than the situation they are in. Never be afraid to say 'no' to someone you are unsure about.

2. *Be careful about bringing people with you who do not look to you pastorally as their leader*

On occasion I have seen people joining a church plant but still looking for their pastoral direction and support to come from a more experienced pastor in a different church. This can lead to complications in due course, since it is very hard for people to look for leadership from one direction and pastoral care from another.

3. *Ensure that expectations are realistic*

Be careful about promising specific positions or roles to members of the team unless you are absolutely sure that they are the right person for the role. It is often better to give someone a smaller job to do and then watch them develop in it than make big appointments up front.

Sometimes potential team members are keen to have a specific role within the church. It is very tempting to promise this or imply that it is likely to come about out of a desire to draw them into the team. However, this can very easily lead to disappointment in due course.

4. *Be careful about recruiting friends*

It can be a very exciting prospect to think of planting a church along with friends, particularly if you have always ministered together as peers up until now.

However, you should be aware that there will be some subtle but very important changes in the dynamics of your relationship if they join a team that you are now leading.

There are times as a leader when you have to put the church or team first and make demands of individuals that you would not make if you were only being their friend. Many friendships cannot take this change in dynamic and one should be wary about inviting close friends to join the church plant. At the very least, make sure you talk about these sorts of issues and how they may affect your relationship before you make a commitment to them joining you.

Starting to build the team together

1. Start to build a sense of community

As people begin to join the team look for opportunities to introduce them to each other and begin to develop a sense of community.

2. Cast vision

Just as you have shared your vision with individuals, now start to share your vision with the group as a whole. This helps to knit the group together as they start to focus around a common sense of purpose.

3. Keep the group open to new people

As you begin to develop a sense of community, make sure that the group gets used to the fact that there will always be new people joining you.

Becoming too focused on building relationships in the core group can cause people to stop looking beyond it. This can be terminal for a church plant! Seek to maintain a fine balance in the early months between getting to know each other and talking about why God has brought you together. Also, keep inviting new people into the group. This starts to develop a sense of momentum that is invaluable to any church plant.

*   *   *

We have considered the vital questions of call, preparation, location, vision and building a team. We now need to focus more closely on the church planter himself.

This second section of this manual will help you consider where you need to grow and develop in order to be ready for the great adventure of planting churches.

Section 2:
The qualities of a
church planter

7

CHARACTERISTICS OF A CHURCH PLANTER

'The LORD has sought out a man after his own heart and appointed him leader of his people ... he will do everything I want him to do.'

said of David in 1 Samuel 13:14 and Acts 13:22

'The most important single factor, apart from the sovereign call of God in church planting, is the suitability of the leader for the task. Make sure you are confident that these qualities apply to you before you launch out!'

Colin Baron, church planter, ChristChurch Manchester

Having taken the very first steps towards starting my first church, I went down with pneumonia and was sick for the next two months. It felt like a wake up call. If I was going to see a church planted it looked like it was going to be a challenging and costly business!

When I started the church in central London the challenges were different, but just as demanding. On this occasion finance was the great challenge – the demand of the enormous amounts of money required to move people into the city, hire venues and do all the other things required to get the church going.

You can be sure that you will face obstacles too as you seek to get a church started. It is always a demanding process, even for those who have done it before.

Planting a church often requires moving home, finding a new job and helping your children get settled into new schools. It requires starting with nothing and going on to create a vibrant, Spirit-filled community! This demands determination, perseverance and a particular set of qualities and abilities if you are to succeed.

Therefore, it is important to ask yourself some hard questions before you start a new church:

- Am I really suited for this, or does God have a different role for me in the body of Christ?

- Has God given me the gifts and abilities I need to do it?

- Is the timing right?

Asking these questions provides a number of advantages:

1. If you conclude that God has gifted you to do it, then you will enter the process with a lot more confidence.

2. It will help you identify your strengths and make the most of them.

3. It will help you identify your weaknesses so that you can give more attention to them and work on improving them.

4. It will help you identify more clearly the other types of gifts that you need on your team.

If you discover that leading a church plant is not for you, then you can continue to seek God for his plans for your life, secure in the knowledge that you have just saved yourself and your family from what could have been a very costly mistake.

A thorough assessment of these issues will also help you avoid some of the unhelpful ways in which church planters can be selected. Sometimes leaders let people go church planting ...

- ... to get rid of a troublesome or un-submissive character.
- ... in the hope that church planting may help them to work on their character issues.
- ... because of a 'holy hunch' or an un-weighed prophetic word.
- ... to avoid having to tell someone that they are not a leader.

Characteristics of a church planter

Here is a list of what I consider to be the essential qualities of a church planter. It is meant to serve as a checklist for those who are considering leading a church plant themselves. A number of the forthcoming chapters develop individual qualities in more detail.

A faith-inspired vision and call

1. Confidence that God has called you

Before starting to plant a church it is essential to know that God has called you to do this. This sense of call can come in many different ways, but it cannot be avoided. Throughout the pages of Scripture God's plans for men and women's lives often start with a specific call to a specific task. God is still doing the same today.

It is important that the church planter is convinced that this is God's will for them. The call of God will keep them going when things are hard, when growth is slow or when key people leave. It is the unshakable conviction that, 'Whatever happens and however things go, God has called me to this.'

'On a dark country road I was overtaken by a drunk driver who hit a motorcyclist head on, throwing him into a field. It took me a good few minutes in the dark to find the motorcyclist who was dead. Confronted with a horrific scene, I found myself asking where this young man had gone — heaven or hell? It was in that moment, and during the subsequent soul searching that followed, that God put a fiery passion in me for starting churches and reaching lost people for Christ.'

Andy Moyle, Gateway Church, King's Lynn

2. *A clear, inspiring vision*

Out of every call flows a vision. This vision will be deeply rooted in what the Scriptures teach us about the church. It will also be powerfully shaped by the things God has spoken to the church planter (and apostolic team) about this church in its specific context.

It will include some idea of the kind of people the church will be reaching, possibly its location, its size and some of the ministries that will be present within it.

The clarity of this vision will be a major factor in drawing the initial church planting team together and will act as a magnet to draw others as the team begins to grow and develop.

3. *A history of taking steps of faith*

Faith is an essential component for the church planter. It is the essential quality needed to create something out of nothing and this is exactly what happens in the creation of a new church. This faith results in remarkable breakthroughs and the provision of amazing resources so that the vision can begin to be fulfilled.

Any would-be church planter should be able to recount previous steps of faith that they have taken, however small. They will prove to have been a great preparation for what is to come.

'My own conviction that I should be involved in planting churches grew from a sense that God had called me. Also, the leaders around me were all confirming this. They were saying, "We think you can do this" and that was very important to me. Several of them had been involved in planting churches and knew what they were looking for in potential church planters. It was the combination of these two things: God's call and the affirmation of leaders who knew me well that gave me the impetus to launch out and have a go.'

A successful church planter

A godly character

4. *A strong spiritual life*

Starting a church plant requires a particular type of leadership: spiritual leadership. In other words, it is essential that you have a strong personal relationship with God and are in the habit of sustaining it with your own times of prayer and study of God's word.

The strength of the spiritual life of the church you develop will, to a greater or lesser extent, be shaped by the strength of your own life with God. Don't go church planting unless your own spiritual life is vital and strong.

'For me, the first criteria for any church planter is that they are secure in God's love and know that they have gained his mercy and favour without having done anything themselves.

This has always been the basis from which I have sought to start new churches. Each time we have planted I've needed to come to God and ask him for fresh grace for the new venture ahead. Then I continue to keep coming to him. As I've asked, he has always supplied what I've needed.

I know that when I have had a clear vision and faith for a strategy, that it has been born out of relationship with God. I know it's the grace of God that has supplied the team with the right gifts for the area we are about to work into. As we have prayed, he has always brought the right people together.

Grace has helped me to understand that just as "one sows and another waters", only God gives the growth. Signs of life take time to appear; for a new church plant to become a family requires a process of growing in the grace of God.

It takes a work of grace for momentum to develop and it may take years to see breakthroughs, so I have learned to stay in the grace of God, enjoy his presence and work hard but not strive. I have also learned to trust that the vision he gave will produce fruit.'

Anthony Henson has planted churches in Orpington, Leicester, Stoke-on-Trent and currently leads, Grace Church, Lincoln

5. *A good marriage*

Church planting brings lots of stresses and strains into a marriage. During the gathering stage especially, you will have countless people through your home; you will sometimes be tired, there will be seasons of spiritual warfare and there will be days when fewer people turn up than you were hoping for!

All of these things can put pressure on your marriage. Don't try church planting unless your marriage is strong.

6. *Personally secure*

Church planting comes with its share of bumps and bruises. Unfortunately, people will disagree with you, criticise you and talk behind your back. People come, but they also leave.

All this requires that church planters have a deep sense of personal security based in what Christ has done for them at the cross and a solid understanding of who they are in Christ. This frees leaders from having to look for man's approval and enables them to make tough, courageous decisions as God leads without fearing how people will respond.

7. *A good follower*

God gives authority to those who function well under authority. Any church planter must have a history of responding well to those whom God has set over them.

> 'The centurion replied, "Lord, I do not deserve to have you come under my roof. But just say the word, and my servant will be healed. For I myself am a man under authority, with soldiers under me. I tell this one, 'Go,' and he goes; and that one, 'Come,' and he comes. I say to my servant, 'Do this,' and he does it." When Jesus heard this, he was astonished and said to those following him, "I tell you the truth, I have not found anyone in Israel with such great faith."'
>
> Matthew 8:8–10

In the same way it is essential that church planters open their lives and their churches to those with apostolic gifts or others who the apostles have asked to serve them.

Counsel and advice from those who have planted churches before is of great benefit and can save you hours of heartache. These people can prevent you heading up blind alleys or making other mistakes that sap the church plant of momentum and fruitfulness.

Possesses key church planting abilities

8. *An ability to win those who do not know Christ*

The primary aim of church planting is to reach lost people and to build them into the church. It is important that the church planter leads by example in this regard by ensuring that he is giving time and energy to building relationships with those who do not know Christ. He will also effectively motivate other members of the team to do the same and create events and other opportunities where members of the team can meet each other's friends.

9. *Effectively builds strong relationships*

To start a church is to create a new community and any new community is based on relationships. The church planter sets the tone for the quality and depth of relationships in the church plant and will spend much of his time meeting new people and seeking to draw them into the community.

This means the church planter must be friendly and hospitable, fun to be with and a good listener who is at home with meeting new people and creating new relationships.

10. *A self-starter who works hard*

Church planting is not for the faint hearted. It requires enormous amounts of drive and hard work. It is not for those who tire easily or lack motivation. In many cases the pioneering leader may be engaged in secular employment whilst starting the church. The church planter will need to set their own goals and manage the steps required to birth the church in their free time, at weekends, early in the morning and late at night.

Even when the church planter is working full time for the church they must be able to manage their own time and achieve the right balance between the hard work needed and maintaining quality time for their marriage, family and replenishing friendships.

11. *An ability to plan, set goals and manage your time*

There is always more to do than there is time to do it – even when you are only working with a relatively small group of people. As a result it is really important that a church planter is able to work out what needs doing at a given time in order to get the church started and then to stick to the plan. It is essential to know which issues are distractions to avoid and which are really opportunities to pursue.

12. *Raise up other leaders*

As the church plant grows you must be able to pass your leadership on to others, so that you can move on to take up the new responsibilities that growth brings with it. This means that you must become familiar with and effective at identifying potential leaders and then training and releasing them into areas of the church plant.

13. *A good communicator*

You need to have the ability to talk in a small group setting and to larger groups, both in terms of communicating general information (what we are doing next week, why we are doing it, where we are doing it, etc) and in terms of preaching and teaching.

*   *   *

I appreciate that reading through such a long list of challenging qualities can be a little dispiriting! If you are struggling to get a good 'read' of yourself (Rom. 12:3), then you could use the content of this chapter as the basis for a discussion with another leader who knows you well. They should be able to help you sort through where you are at and what God is saying to you.

Having got something of an overview of the qualities needed for church planting, we are now ready to examine some of those qualities in more detail.

8

PLANNING AND GOAL SETTING

' "For I know the plans I have for you," declares the LORD, "plans to prosper you and not to harm you, plans to give you hope and a future." '

Jeremiah 29:11

'In him we were also chosen, having been predestined according to the plan of him who works out everything in conformity with the purpose of his will.'

Ephesians 1:11

'From the east I summon ... a man to fulfil my purpose. What I have said, that will I bring about; what I have planned, that will I do.'

Isaiah 46:11

'To the person who does not know where he wants to go there is no favourable wind.'

Seneca

For me to stay focused on the things that God wants me to do is an ongoing challenge. There are so many other opportunities, needs and distractions that come my way! It is just the same for any Christian leader and particularly for any church planter.

At the start of each New Year I typically spend some time reviewing the previous year and thinking about the year to come. During this time I will reflect on any prophetic direction that God has given and seek to synchronise that with other things that I believe God has put on my heart for the coming year.

I will then draw up a plan for the year. This is a document that highlights the key things I believe God is asking me to do in the coming twelve months and the implications of that in terms of people I need to work with, new areas that God is asking me to believe him for breakthrough in, and new growth that God is asking of me personally.

Based on this document I then prayerfully decide what I particularly need to focus on in the coming month. In other words, I decide what I am going to do in January in light of the goals I believe God has given me for the whole year.

Then, at the start of each successive month, I think about where things are at and set goals for the coming thirty days. I often find myself looking at what I've drawn up. It tells me what progress I am making, reminds me what I should be focusing on and keeps my eyes lifted to the breadth of God's plans as well as the details of the moment.

For me, this combination of hearing God and implementing what he is saying with planning and goal setting is essential to staying fruitful and energised as each month of a year comes and goes.

Joseph is a great example of a biblical leader who used similar skills to bless a whole nation (Gen. 41:25–57). He combined prophetic direction, goal setting and planning in his handling of the famine that hit Egypt.

Prophetic direction came through his interpretation of Pharaoh's dreams.

His goal setting and planning skills were shown as he directed Pharaoh to put aside 20% of the harvest each year during the good years, so that there would be enough to get the nation through the fallow years that would follow.

It is important that we also learn to combine these twin tools of prophetic direction and planning. We should not see them as being in opposition to one another. Rather, planning helps us to be responsible in ensuring that we actually get done the things that God has been talking to us about!

The combination of these two elements of leadership can prove to be very powerful in the hands of a godly leader. Prophetic revelation often brings great inspiration and then planning and implementation saves people from the frustration that arises if nothing happens after God has spoken.

What do we mean by planning?

Planning aims to anticipate the growth and development of the church over a given period of time, taking into account the vision and prophetic direction that God has given you.

It is a valuable tool to be used for the development of the church as a whole and for the development of various projects and ministries within the life of the church.

When you are starting a church it makes a great difference to actually write your plan down. You will be amazed how much clearer you are forced to be, just by putting your thoughts down on paper. Also, fellow leaders will be able to see what you are planning, what is required of them and how they can contribute.

> '*If you aim at nothing, you are sure to hit it.*'
>
> Unknown

How do you balance planning and flexibility?

There is a real balance to achieve here, because both of these qualities are important in a pioneering situation.

Planning provides consistency. The church plant will need that. The people will need to know that when the leader says, 'We are going this way ...' that it is indeed the case. Church plants cannot cope with many changes of direction!

Equally, for some planning can become a straight jacket. Nobody wants to be slavishly devoted to a plan that has become irrelevant, out of date or is just plain wrong. We must constantly bear in mind that planning is a tool to serve us and must be submitted to the ongoing leading of the Spirit.

This combination gives us both flexibility and a clear sense of direction.

'*When an aeroplane embarks on a journey, the destination and flight route are clear before the pilot takes off. However, during the flight he has to make constant minor readjustments to ensure that the plane remains on course. We should not be afraid to show the same flexibility with regard to our plans.*'

Matt Hatch, Mosaic Church, Leeds

Flexibility is also important. Nobody can predict the future. There are always going to be unexpected events, great opportunities to take hold of or crises to respond to. At times like these we must be able to respond with speed and agility. This means the plans we have must be held lightly.

What are the benefits of planning?

1. *It turns your vision into practical, action-orientated steps*

A plan shows you what you need to do to move towards bringing the vision about. It should answer the question, 'What do I need to do today in order that we take steps towards our ultimate vision?'

> 'Suppose one of you wants to build a tower. Will he not first sit down and estimate the cost to see if he has enough money to complete it? For if he lays the foundation and is not able to finish it, everyone who sees it will ridicule him, saying, "This fellow began to build and was not able to finish."'
>
> Luke 14:28–30

2. *It helps you see the challenges and obstacles ahead of time*

Thoughtful and thorough planning anticipates obstacles ahead of time, enabling you to prepare properly for them. These obstacles are invariably easier to overcome with some planning and forethought ahead of time.

If, for instance, you are starting the church plant in January and are hoping to have three small groups by April, then you have to be asking yourself well in advance, 'Where am I going to get three small group leaders from?' This forces you to either start training people as soon as you begin the church plant or make sure you recruit three small group leaders to be part of your team before you start.

3. *It helps you make decisions more quickly*

The planning process anticipates many of the decisions that you need to make as you progress. By thinking things through ahead of time you have less to work out on the run and can concentrate on your relationships with God, your family and those you are gathering, secure in the knowledge that you are heading in the right direction.

4. *It helps keep you focused*

It is easy to start something with great enthusiasm, but to lose that sense of energy and drive as time goes by and other issues take up your attention.

Life becomes busy, other demands distract us and we lose motivation. All of these things mean that we can lose our focus if we are not careful. A plan helps to keep us on course.

There are some days when there are so many things to pray for it is hard to know where to start! At times like this it can be helpful to get out your plan and begin to pray about the things you need to be doing immediately, as well as the big challenges to come.

'I remember asking Bill Hybels a question about vision and strategy. He said, "Howard, if you're great at casting vision but you haven't got a plan, then sooner or later your people will realise you are just blowing smoke."'

Howard Kellet, Hope Church, Manchester

What should you plan?

Before the church plant starts, you should be looking to develop a plan for the whole church. This plan should cover the first one–two years of the church plant and should involve every area of the church's life.

In the early days of a church plant it is hard to see too far ahead. One can probably only do detailed planning up to about six months ahead. The six months after that have less detail and the plan for the following year probably consists more of a broad outline of where you hope to be.

Once you are through the first couple of years you will be able to plan further ahead, but in the early days this is more difficult.

> 'The most common mistake leaders make when they plan is to overestimate what they can accomplish in one year and under-estimate what they can accomplish in five years.'

How do you plan?

One of the most effective ways to begin the planning process is by asking a series of questions and writing out the answers. These questions should include:

1. Where are we now?

If you are going to create a plan to get you to a particular destination it is crucial that you are clear about where you are starting from! Be totally honest. Where are things at? What are the strengths and weaknesses of your current position?

'A plan of the future based on a unrealistic view of the present will lead to disaster.'

2. *Where are we going?*

Clearly, the ultimate destination is shaped by the vision of the church, but for the sake of the planning process the answer can be shaped by different time scales: six months, one year, three years and five years.

3. *How do we get there?*

To put this another way, ask yourself ...

- 'What am I going to do between arriving in town and starting a Sunday meeting?'
- 'How am I going to meet unbelievers and those who are looking for a church?'
- 'Who are the key people I need to recruit?'
- 'What ministries do I need to start and what venues do I need to find?'
- 'How much money will we need each month and how are we going to get it?'

As you identify the chief areas that you need to focus on it can be helpful to set goals that are:

S.M.A.R.T.

- *Specific:* what precisely are you aiming at?
- *Measurable:* how will you know when you have achieved it?
- *Agreed:* not just 'my goal' but a goal that everyone in the team has taken ownership of.

- *Realistic:* with faith, can you believe God for it?
- *Time-tabled:* when will you have achieved it by?

This should then answer the questions:

- What do you need to do now?
- What support will you need along the way?
- What obstacles are you most likely to face?
- What three things must I do if this is to succeed?

'Goals which are formed by determining the ideal long term destination and then setting out the realistic steps towards achieving it are more inspiring, creative and motivating. We are not just looking for merely short term gains, but a clear picture of the long term goals that fit the vision of the church. Goals must be concrete and measurable steps that, if accomplished, will bring the vision into reality.'[1]

Steve Nicholson, Coaching Church Planters

'Each year I have set seven clear and measurable goals for the church. They have always been slightly beyond our abilities, but achievable with a mix of faith and hard work.

Most goals have been very simple such as, "Have fifty people attending our Sunday meeting each week by June" or "Run three Alpha courses, one per term" or "Baptise at least ten people this year", but they have always covered the basic things that I believed we needed to do to plant a healthy church.

On a Sunday evening at the start of each term I will share with everyone what this year's priorities are, with an inspirational presentation including progress updates, photos and a public celebration of successes. I will also aim to relate all our goals to any prophecy that has come during the year and take time to talk about the goals that we have not yet reached. In each of our three years we have hit all seven of our goals by December and exceeded most of them.

This approach has helped me as a leader to stay focused and intentional and has helped church members to know where to focus their energy and prayers. It has also meant we have been able to see where we have been successful and to celebrate what God has done.'

Steve Petch, Grace Church, Chichester

4. *How are we doing?*

You should be regularly comparing your current progress against the plan and asking, 'How are we doing?' Constant evaluation is a necessity.

Sometimes this results in making significant changes to what you are doing.

You have to have the courage to stop the things that are not working and start new things in the hope that they will work. Not to do this is to invite failure.

Ongoing planning

Planning is not something that should only be done as the church is starting, but is a useful tool any time one starts to develop a new aspect of the life of the church.

Any time that you start anything you will find it helpful to ask the following questions:

'*Who* will do it?'
'*What* is it that I am asking them to do?'
'*When* do I want them to start?'
'*Where* are they going to be doing this?'
'*How* will they go about doing it?'

Answering these questions and seeing through on the required action will smooth the way to starting any new ministry in the church.

*   *   *

There is a 'partner' to planning which makes it effective and that is the ability to manage your time. If you are going to make your planning happen you have to ensure that you are spending your time in the right way. This is the subject of the next chapter where we look at how we can use our time most effectively, ensuring that we get to do the things that God is asking us to do.

9

STAYING FOCUSED: MANAGING YOUR TIME AS A CHURCH PLANTER

'I am carrying on a great project and cannot go down. Why should the work stop while I leave it and go down to you?'

Nehemiah 6:3

'The thing that I lose patience with the most is the clock. Its hands move too fast. Time is really the only capital that any human being has and the one thing he can least afford to waste or lose.'

Thomas Edison

Some years ago I sat in on a conversation between a young church planter and an apostolic leader who was trying to help him develop his church plant. The young leader was evidently frustrated: 'I have around forty people in my church plant,' he said, 'and now I do not have any time to meet any new people. The needs of these forty people take up all my time!'

The seasoned leader leaned forward. 'Here's what I suggest you do,' he said. 'Divide your time in half. Give 50% of it to the people you already have and give the other 50% to finding the next forty people.'

The church planter took the advice quite literally. He went through his diary for the coming months and simply wrote the words 'new people' across 50% of his working time. He was not sure yet what he was going to do with that time, but he knew he would spend it on reaching those who were not yet part of the church plant. If anyone else asked for that time he could say, with sincerity, that it was already booked.

In those few moments that young pioneer learned one of the key benefits of managing his time. Taking control of his diary meant he now had time to do the things that were most important to his ministry (and for the future of the church). He was no longer simply responding to what others wanted him to do.

Managing your time matters

1. *God has given us time, we are to steward it properly*

Many leaders fritter their time away with badly organised schedules, by attending meetings that do not take things forward, and by spending time on the wrong things.

In the end we will have to account to God for the way in which we have used our time.

Therefore, we should ensure we spend our time on the things that really matter. Taking God's kingdom forward, enjoying being with those we love and making the most of the gifts and abilities that God has given us are all important parts of this.

2. *Managing your time is particularly important if you are planting a church*

Every church plant has a finite amount of time to develop into a fully established church. After a particular point, momentum is lost, expectancy declines and confidence in the leadership begins to wane.

This is why it is critical that the church planter learns to use their time effectively. If they become sidetracked and spend too much of their time doing the wrong things, then the people they have gathered are likely to begin to disperse and the church plant is likely to die.

3. *Managing your time well makes space for you to exercise leadership, to be proactive and to make things happen*

When leaders give their time to the things that really matter they function in the way that they should – they take initiative and are not simply responding to events of other's making.

In a church plant this means initiating gathering events, inviting people over for food, meeting up with potential leaders and meeting new people. The church planter makes time for these things by ensuring that he is getting other things done efficiently and effectively.

4. *Managing your time well enables you to do more of what you want to do*

A leader who manages his time well has more time for prayer and study, more time for the people he loves and more time to do the things he is passionate about doing. This means that he is also more effective in the ministry God has given him.

How do we go about managing our time?

1. *Be clear on what your priorities are*

Once you have developed your plan you will be clear about the things that you must give your time to for the church plant to succeed.

You need to write these down somewhere – on your desk, in your dairy or on the desktop of your computer – so that you can look at them on a daily basis.

Your task is to stick to these priorities and start to make them happen.

When I was planting my first church, I found that it was a real challenge to stay focused on the things that would take us forward. There was always another email to be returned, another phone call to make or someone else who wanted to meet up. It was easy to stay busy without ever asking, 'What should I be doing today that will take us forward?' In the end I put a card on my desk that read, 'The main thing, is to keep the main thing, the main thing'. This helped me not to get distracted by simply being busy and ensured that I was doing what really mattered.

2. Be clear on the difference between the 'urgent' and the 'important'

It is easy to get so busy that you stop asking whether what you are doing is really important. Each event needs to be organised; people need to be befriended and cared for; but the whirl of activity can make it difficult to make any sort of analysis of what you are doing and whether it matters.

Every now and then you need to step back and ask, 'Is this *important* or is it simply *urgent*?'

'Urgent' and 'important' are not always the same thing. A ringing phone is urgent, it demands our immediate attention, but it may not make any long term difference to your life or the life of the church plant.

Important matters, on the other hand, are things that if left unattended will have significant consequences. You might not notice the impact of leaving them undone for some months, but ultimately they will have a serious affect on your ability to take the church forward.

As we learn to manage our time we learn to ensure that we give time each day to the important matters.

3. Have a daily 'to do' list in which you identify which items are most important

A daily to do list helps keep you focused and ensures that you are getting the right things done today.

Also make sure you are clear on what the most important things are on your list. Otherwise, it is tempting to start with the easiest or most appetising and you will find that the most important, but more difficult items, are still left undone at the end of the day.

4. Ensure that you keep some flexibility in your schedule so that you can respond to the promptings of the Spirit as well as unexpected opportunities that arise

In the first 12–24 months you want to spend as much of your time as possible with people, and evenings and weekends are the best times for this. Keep as much of this time free for people as possible.

5. Block out time ahead in your diary to ensure that the important things get done

As the church plant grows, life has to become more organised. Make sure that you put blocks of time into your schedule for study and preparation.

6. Learn to say 'no'

Every church planter and church leader faces times when they have to say 'no'. Even Jesus did this:

'Very early in the morning, while it was still dark, Jesus got up, left the house and went off to a solitary place, where he prayed. Simon and his companions went to look for him, and when they found him, they exclaimed: "Everyone is looking for you!" Jesus replied, "Let us go somewhere else — to the nearby villages — so I can preach there also. That is why I have come."'

Mark 1:35–38

Without this skill we will end up being men pleasers rather than those who please God. This can easily result in us damaging our families and our ministries.

A reminder: three things you must keep doing

Here are three church planting essentials that you need to stay focused on:

1. *Are you casting vision regularly?*

Keep telling people where you are going. Stay excited and energised about it yourself. Spending time praying for what God will do in the future helps enormously in this.

Give time to regularly refining your vision so that it becomes clearer as the church develops.

2. *Are you meeting new people?*

When did you last meet someone new? How many new people have you met over the last month?

Care for those you have already gathered, but do not allow them to take up so much time that you cannot get to the next people who need to be drawn in.

3. Are you training leaders?

This takes time. Leaders are not made in a day. The sooner you can start and the more intentional you are, the more fruitful you will be and the more leaders the church will have.

*   *   *

In this section we have focused on the use of our time, primarily with regard to the leadership of the church plant. This is critical; time is your most important asset and you must use it wisely. However, there is another group of people who really need your time as well – your family. It's time to focus on them in the next section.

10

MAKING SURE THE FAMILY THRIVE WHILST PLANTING A CHURCH

'Greet Priscilla and Aquila, my fellow-workers in Christ Jesus. They risked their lives for me. Not only I but all the churches of the Gentiles are grateful to them. Greet also the church that meets at their house.'

Romans 16:3–5

'Each one of you also must love his wife as he loves himself, and the wife must respect her husband ... Fathers, do not exasperate your children; instead, bring them up in the training and instruction of the Lord.'

Ephesians 5:33; 6:4

Whilst we were planting the church in Birmingham, both Philippa and I found that we were travelling more away from home, often getting back late and leaving early in the morning. This was at a time when the children were still quite young.

With life being so busy it was really important to us that the children knew there was a time each week when we would have time together as a family and that this time would not be interrupted by other people wanting our attention.

As a result we instituted a family 'video and popcorn night' on a Friday evening. The children knew that every Friday we would sit down together as a family, have our supper in front of a film of their choice and eat popcorn. The phones would be turned off, emails ignored and callers invited to join us for the film or to catch up at another time.

Though the films we watch together have changed, the Stroud 'video and popcorn night' has run for many years and is still a time for us all to kick back, turn off the phones, eat food and enjoy being together!

Not all church planters have children at home. Some may be single, others may be yet to start a family, and others will be 'empty nesters'. Nevertheless, whatever stage of life you are in, church planting brings unusual pressures on home life and it is very important that the church planter is prepared for these and has started to think through how to handle them.

Church planting and an open home

1. *Most church planters find that the most effective way to gather people is to invite them into their home*

This really strengthens the sense of connection between new people and the leader and helps prospective members feel that they are getting to know the church planter and his family.

2. *The church planter should expect to have scores of people through his home in the first few years*

This is not only for organised events, but also people simply dropping by when they are passing. In fact, there is normally a correlation between the number of people who join the church in the first year or two and the number of people who have come through the church planter's home.

Many church planters thrive in this sort of environment and love the feeling of being at the centre of the action. However, it also brings particular pressures that is important to be aware of.

3. *The pressures of an open home include:*

- *Late nights.* You want to encourage people to feel at home and stay as long as they would like after a meeting, but once they have left there is clearing up to be done and other jobs that need to be finished off before the start of the next day.

- For many church planters, this is not a once a week occurrence but, for a season, happens on the majority of evenings in a week. Week after week this can take its toll on a leader's health, energy levels and spiritual life.

- *People dropping by unexpectedly.* Visitors do not always arrive at convenient times! Sometimes, there is a knock on the door as you are tired, busy, or in the middle of dealing with a family conflict. This can also prove to be a great energy sapper.

- *Time together as a couple.* With all the other time demands, it is a constant challenge to ensure you have sufficient time for the ingredients of a healthy marriage: unhurried time together to talk, have fun and enjoy being together.

- *Children feeling they do not have enough of their parents' attention.* The demands of work, meeting new people, training leaders and ensuring you are on top of the jobs around the house can easily mean that the

children feel they are not having the time that they
need with their Mum and Dad.

- *Wear and tear on the furniture.* High levels of
  hospitality impact the home. Carpets and soft
  furnishings feel the strain and countless mugs
  for tea and coffee need to be stored and replaced
  regularly!

*'For the children to thrive during the church planting phase it is really
important that you know each of them well. Different personality
types respond differently to a given situation, so understanding your
child's personality will enable you to help them deal with events at
home or church. For example, one of our children is an introvert and
needs time by himself to recharge his batteries. If we have a lot of
people through the house he can get tired and upset. I chat with him
beforehand and tell him that if he gets tired to come and talk to me,
rather than complain. He has started to recognize when he is getting
"peopled-out", so he now comes to tell me he needs a bit of time by
himself and takes himself off to his bedroom. One of our other children
loves looking after people and so we have given her the job of talking
to any new children in church and helping them feel welcome. Being
aware of each child's personality has helped us ensure our children
have stayed loving God and loving his church.'*

Pip Hatch, Mosaic Church, Leeds

Strong foundations are required to handle the pressures and joys of an open home

1. *Do not go church planting unless your marriage is strong and your children are in a good place*

Church planting is spiritual warfare and we can expect to
be opposed by the devil (1 Pet. 5:8). He will seek to attack
us where we are weak.

It brings no glory to God to embark on a project for him and then for our marriage to falter or our children to begin to resent God or their parents for what they have been through.

2. *Prepare yourself for a more demanding season, but know when it is going to come to an end*

Whenever we have started a new church we have talked together about the fact that, for a season, life will get very busy and we will not have quite as much spare time as we have had previously.

Our main goal in discussing this together as a family is to get some level of 'buy in' from everyone. We have often been surprised how well we can manage for a while, as long as we know that a more relaxed pace is coming in due course.

3. *Make sure your wife and children know that they are more important to you than the church plant*

Even though everyone may recognise that this is going to be a busy period, it is still essential that your family know that their wellbeing matters more than that of the church plant.

'Philippa and I have gone to enormous ends to make it clear to our children that they come first. There have been times where we have cancelled meetings, re-worked our schedule and not taken up exciting ministry opportunities because we have not felt that the children were ready for the demands it would make on us as a family.

Though we take responsibility for monitoring the "pace" of life, we have also encouraged our children to tell us when they feel the busyness is becoming too much or when they could do with more of our time and attention.'

David Stroud

4. Draw the children into the adventure

Church planting is a wonderfully exciting adventure and as the children grow you can share more and more of this with them. The best way to parent your children is to model a life of faith, following the calling of God on your own life.

'We moved from The Coign, a large church with 500 members in Woking, to plant a church in Camberley with twelve other people. Our three boys were one, four and six years old.

The whole process was a massive challenge. The children particularly felt the impact of leaving their friends behind and I had to really hang on to God's promises for each of them.

Mark has been brilliant in the way he has led the family and kept our spiritual life strong together, and we have made sure our children love their own home and are comfortable bringing friends of any description into it. One of my sons calls us the "special church family, because new people like to come to our house."

Also, we got each of the boys serving in the church as early as we could and encouraged them to tell us how they think things are going and what could be done better. This has helped them to really feel part of things and to know that they have their own contribution as well.'

Bev Landreth-Smith, Beacon Church, Camberley, Surrey

Teenagers in particular do not want a life that is predictable and conventional, but rather something that has an element of 'risk' about it. They like living on the edge. Church planting gives them a taste of this and shows how following Jesus can be a full on, exciting adventure!

5. Do not put expectations on your children to set an example that you would not expect from other people's children

As church plant leaders it can be very easy to feel that your children must be a model for how everyone else's children should behave, whether it is in their engagement in worship, their attendance in the children's work or the level of their spiritual life.

Do not put your children under this sort of pressure. They need to be able to be themselves. We have constantly sought to allow our children to grow at their own pace, with their own level of maturity, without asking them to become 'model children' along the way.

Children have enough challenges to cope with without feeling that they have to live up to a certain image of being the leader's children as well.

6. *Given the fact that so many of the meetings you will have in the first couple of years will be in your home, look for a house that can cater for the needs of a growing family as well as a growing church!*

These may include:

- *Enough downstairs space.* We have always sought to live in homes that are set out in such a way that the children are not consigned to their bedrooms if we have evening meetings in the house. As they get older this becomes particularly important.

- *Space for parties and gathering events.* Does the home have enough space so that you can have a crowd around?

- *A dedicated workspace within the home* (assuming that you cannot afford to have a church office at this point in time) where you can think, pray, prepare, etc. If this is not possible, make sure that you invest in a laptop and wireless network so that you can always find a quiet space to be productive somewhere in the house.

Enjoying family life during the gathering stage

1. *Make sure that you have times when you get out, get away and turn the phone off*

Jesus would get away to spend time with his Father when the crowds were out looking for him (Mark 1:37). It is very important that we too are not afraid to leave the crowds for a time to be by ourselves and with our families.

It is also OK to tell a spontaneous visitor that this is not a good time to call and suggest another time when you can get together.

2. *Enjoy nights out, weekends away and holidays*

It is very easy to become so focused on planting a church that you forget that there is another area of your life where you need to take initiative, be creative and organise some great events – this time for the family!

Look for special offers, develop leisure activities that you enjoy doing as a whole family and try and budget as much as possible for family holidays.

Some years ago good friends of ours said to us, 'We have decided to budget more for family holidays than most people do. As we look back on our childhood it is the family holidays that stand out as being the most memorable parts of our growing up years. We want to create great memories for our children and so we have decided to do our best to invest in holidays in the same way.' We thought this was great advice and have sought to do the same, where we can, ever since.

3. *Working from home*

If you are working 'full time' for the church based at home then ensure the family understands what your 'office hours' are. This will enable you to get on with the things you have to do and enables the family to be clear on when you will be available for them.

4. *Remember to pace yourself differently at different times of the year*

Some parts of the church year are much busier than others and we must learn to correlate this with the needs of family life.

We know that there are times when things will be very 'full on', but that other periods of the year will be less demanding, so we must make a conscious decision to particularly invest in our lives together as a family during these quieter seasons.

I often think that parenting is not unlike long term leadership training! As I invest in my children and pour my life into theirs, I trust that they will become natural initiative takers and leaders themselves.

* * *

When we are church planting we are training at another level as well: our future effectiveness will be shaped by the leaders we are able to raise up around us. It is to this subject of raising leaders that we now turn.

11

RAISING UP OTHER LEADERS

'Even though you have ten thousand guardians in Christ, you do not have many fathers, for in Christ Jesus I became your father through the gospel. Therefore I urge you to imitate me. For this reason I am sending to you Timothy, my son whom I love, who is faithful in the Lord. He will remind you of my way of life in Christ Jesus, which agrees with what I teach everywhere in every church.'

The Apostle Paul, 1 Corinthians 4:15–17

'Jesus went up on a mountainside and called to him those he wanted, and they came to him. He appointed twelve – designating them apostles – that they might be with him and that he might send them out to preach.'

Mark 3:13–14

'The function of leadership is to produce more leaders, not more followers.'

Ralph Nadar

Whilst I was thinking about how I should fill the months between school and university, my pastor, David Devenish, said to me, 'Why don't we spend a month together? You can arrive at my house at 6.30 a.m. each morning and work through with me until the end of the day. You can join me for my times of prayer, sit in on the counselling sessions, help me with my preparation and learn from my meetings with other leaders.'

I was thrilled to get the opportunity and it proved to be a very significant month for me. I felt as if I was growing on a daily basis during those weeks. There were lots of opportunities to ask David questions and I felt that my heart was being shaped and changed as he shared with me his concerns and hopes for the church. Our times of prayer were particularly memorable as I learnt more about how to worship and intercede, and David's post meeting analyses of how things had gone each Sunday were insightful and perceptive. I was learning what it meant for leadership to be more 'caught than taught'.

In years to come, I also had the privilege of learning to lead alongside David as a fellow elder at Woodside Church in Bedford. During those years he supplemented the opportunities I'd already had with constructive feedback and insights into my leadership, and suggestions as to how I could do things better that helped me to see and concentrate on my strengths.

This was the core of the training that I received as a leader: learning to serve another, observe him, do things on his behalf, gain his constructive feedback and encouragement, and take more responsibility as a result.

I learned in lots of other ways as well. I read lots of books, listened to hundreds of hours of lectures and sermons and received exposure to a wide range of different settings and leadership styles, but all of these supplemented the core training of working alongside another leader.

This, of course, was Jesus' model of training leaders as well. He drew twelve to be 'with him' (Mark 3:14) and then trained them to preach the gospel, heal the sick and cast out demons as he did.

It is this drawing alongside that is the very best way of training other emerging leaders in a church planting situation and it is a critical skill to learn at an early stage.

Why is training leaders so important?

1. *Training leaders allows for the expansion of the embryonic church*

If you do not train leaders, the church plant will get stuck.

As new people come in, they take up the spare capacity that you and the rest of the church plant team have for building relationships and running the events you are putting on. In other words, everyone gets busy just getting to know each other, caring for each other and running the church programme.

This is why it is so important to be training leaders. It is these men and women who can start new small groups, establish ministries and release you from the organisational burden of the developing church.

2. *Training leaders gives an opportunity for others with potential to grow and develop*

Potential leaders will join your church plant and stay with you if there are opportunities to grow. As you release ministry to others you will find that there is a double win: the church begins to grow and so do these new leaders.

Also, it means that you keep them. Leaders with potential who do not get given fresh challenges tend to find their way to fresh pastures.

I do everything I can to avoid leaders being under utilised. I would hate to think they were getting bored or not feeling stretched! So I am always on the lookout for fresh opportunities and challenges for them.

3. *Training anticipates the needs of the future*

Leaders always have one eye on the horizon. They seek to anticipate the future and ensure they are prepared for it.

The best leaders, therefore, do not wait for a shortage of other leaders before they start training. Rather they make training part of their lifestyle, knowing that as the church grows they will have ready trained leaders prepared to take responsibility because they started by anticipating the needs of the future.

4. *Training is necessary to cope with the inevitable 'turnover' of leadership*

Leadership turnover is caused by people moving on, the changing seasons of life, people needing a break and so on. Leaders do not stay still, they are always growing and changing and developing. So are their work and family situations. As a result, there is always a certain amount of transition going on.

Leaders who do not prepare for this turnover often have to appeal to people to continue with their responsibilities when, in reality, they should be taking a break. This can easily result in leaders burning out or resenting the service they are giving to the church.

Who should you train?

1. *Those with good character*

Character is the most important quality in any leader. Without this they will constantly undermine their own credibility by what they do or what they say.

If you have two leaders, one of whom has good character and one who has great gifting, always give more time and responsibility to the one with the stronger character. He is likely to be with you for longer and to make a bigger contribution along the way.

Also, keep your eye out for those who are willing to change and grow. Their character might not be as well polished as others, but if they are genuinely ready to put the hard graft into personal change then they may well become really effective leaders in the church.

2. *Those with potential*

Keep your eye out for those with untapped potential. Many people can play a leading role but do not know what they are capable of. It is our job as leaders to identify their potential and start to draw it out of them.

It is wonderful to watch people discover that they can do more than they ever dreamt they could as other leaders encourage them and believe in them.

3. *Those who are available*

Time availability is important. It is no good starting to train a terrifically able individual who is not able to make many of the meetings because of the demands of work or other commitments.

4. *Those you have faith for*

God gives us faith for some in particular and this is often a signal that we should invest in these people. Not every leader might have faith for them, but when God puts them on your heart then you should look for every opportunity to encourage and disciple them.

5. *Those who are showing they are enthusiastic and committed*

Look for those who are turning up early, staying late and communicating in other ways, 'we are with you'.

Remember that it is much easier to give people new skills and understanding than it is to give them zeal. It is hard to motivate the unmotivated, but very fulfilling to train those who are red hot but do not know what to do!

'When we planted into Leicester in 1997 we also had an aim to plant from there into Derby and Loughborough within a few years, so we were looking for potential leaders right from the start.

The most critical element in raising leaders, I learned, was the way in which I lived myself. I found that young leaders listened acutely, picking up on words, comments and attitudes that I expressed. I had to learn to be wise in the way I lived, knowing that I was quite likely to hear my words repeated by others and my strengths and weaknesses duplicated by them as well.

As we identified potential leaders we would always give them freedom to have a go. It didn't matter if they failed sometimes; this was all part of the learning process. We ensured that they had some support and accountability along the way to help them learn and keep going.'

Anthony Henson, Grace Church, Lincoln

How do you train leaders?

For Jesus, training and building relationship went hand in hand. However, Jesus functioned at different levels of intimacy with different people.

First, he had the seventy-two, a larger crowd that he had trained. Then there were the twelve apostles who he had called to be 'with him' (Mark 3:14). Then, even within the twelve, there was an inner core of three, Peter, James and

John, who Jesus took with him on some occasions. Then we are told that there was one disciple particularly whom 'Jesus loved' (John 13:23).

You can see a similar dynamic working with the apostle Paul. He had a larger team whose composition often changed as he worked with different people, then he had a few with whom he worked more closely, and then he had Timothy with whom he seemed to have a particularly close relationship. Certainly Timothy had spent a lot of time with Paul, for Paul was able to say that Timothy knew *'my way of life in Christ'* (1 Cor. 4:17) and Paul spoke of him as his 'son'.

What I want to underline here is the personal nature of the relationship when it comes to training. Just as the disciples had been 'with Jesus', so Timothy had 'been with' Paul. It is important that we bear this in mind as we start to train other leaders in the church planting context.

Here are some points to consider as you look to train others:

1. You should choose those who you want to train

Do not feel that you have to ask for volunteers (Mark 3:13) and do not feel pressurised by those who want to be close to you. Rather, decide who you want to invest in and give time to these people. It is important that we keep that sense of freedom to draw those we want to us, just as Jesus did.

2. Look for opportunities to minister to those you are training (Matt. 10:8)

Something important happens when you minister to someone and their life changes as a result. They will often look to your leadership more as a result.

'One of my first experiences of leadership was to direct a team of a dozen people who were giving a year to pioneering evangelism as part of starting a new congregation of Woodside Church in Bedford. Before the start of our year an experienced leader took me aside and gave me this advice regarding the team: "Why don't you take a few risks?" he said. "Go on, call down the Holy Spirit on them every now and then and see what happens."

As a result of that advice I kept a close eye out for opportunities to minister to those I was leading. We had some wonderful times when the Holy Spirit fell and really ministered to members of the team. I know that it was as a result of some of those times of prayer and ministry that people's lives changed and my leadership and authority grew in their lives as a result.'

David Stroud

3. *Ask those you are training to do simple tasks (Matt. 14:19)*

Do not be afraid to ask new leaders to start by doing simple tasks that give them an opportunity to serve and give you an opportunity to see their diligence and faithfulness.

John Wimber used to tell how people would come to him wanting to 'serve his ministry'. He said that on a number of occasions he asked them to spend the first six months sweeping out the worship auditorium. If they balked at this he would ask them, 'If you cannot clean up a room, how are you going to clean up men and women's lives?'

4. *Get those you are training to watch you lead (Matt. 5:21–42)*

The best way to teach someone how to pick up a new skill is to show them how to do it first. That is why it is so important to model how to lead before asking others to do it.

This is particularly important in the early days of the church plant as leaders come from other settings. Do not assume that just because they have led somewhere else that they will do things in the way that you want.

If the way in which they are going to do something is important, then make sure they have seen you do it first.

5. *Ask those you are training to go and exercise leadership and then tell you how it has gone (Matt. 10:1; Mark 6:30)*

One of the most powerful experiences for me, in terms of my growth, has been getting feedback from others. It has not always been easy to hear, but it has often been helpful in terms of identifying areas that I need to grow in.

As we develop leaders it is important that we give them the benefit of that kind of feedback ourselves. Make sure there are times when you hand over to others and you take the opportunity to watch how they do. Then, do not miss the opportunity to encourage them and tell them where they were strong and help them where they did not do so well.

'Hope Church Manchester started with a raw but enthusiastic core of twenty somethings. A clear vision helped to focus that energy, but for us to be effective our potential leaders needed training. At first the training was very organic. I would simply involve as many people as I could in what I was doing. Over coffee with potential leaders or in smaller groups I would lay out an outline strategy or bounce the draft diary off them and allow them to discuss it. At prayer meetings we would pray through the stages of the outreach strategy or the nuts and bolts of our Sunday meetings. In those first two years everyone felt like a leader and ownership was high because I was aiming to equip everyone.

Later, as the church grew, training leaders remained central to my role but became more formal and targeted – as a component of our deacons meetings (for those leading small groups and ministries), as a part of smaller discipleship groups that I would gather, and as part of the practical and doctrinal modules of our Hope Intensive Training Series (HITS).

This year, after sending off our fourth lead planter and over twenty others to pioneering church plant teams, it is clear that we created a great context in which people could learn.'

Howard Kellett, Hope Church, Manchester

6. *In time, commission them in their own right (Matt. 28:18–20)*

As the training cycle nears completion it is important that we make it clear what they are now leading, where they are free to take initiative and where they need to check with you before taking things further.

Other issues

1. *Believe in those you train*

There is nothing more powerful than believing in someone you are training. Communicate this through what you say to them and how you act with them. It is amazing what a difference it can make to your leaders when they know that you love them and believe in them.

2. *Do not sidestep confrontation when it is necessary*

Scripture often encourages us to 'admonish' one another (Col. 3:16; 1 Thess. 5:12), but it is important that we do this carefully and sensitively.

Here are some pointers to bear in mind if you need to give some feedback to one of your leaders:

- Always start with the positive
- Always give the benefit of the doubt
- Avoid absolutes. Use language such as, 'this is how you came across ... this was my impression ...' This gives them an opportunity to respond and clarify what they were trying to do, to correct an impression, to explain their motives and so on.
- Always seek to work things through to a resolution – even if it means suggesting they go away and reflect on what you have said so that you can talk again in due course.
- Don't quote other people's opinions unless they are present. It is very hard to hear what others think if there is no way of responding to them. Keep your feedback personal wherever possible.

3. Do not overestimate your mentoring/training skills

Sometimes leaders can be over optimistic in terms of the amount of change they think they can work in someone's life. A coach can bring the best out in a sportsperson, but the sportsperson must have some natural hand-eye coordination first. In the same way, we can shape the leaders God brings to us, but we should not expect to create leaders out of those who do not have any leadership gifting in the first place.

4. Remember, adults learn best on a 'need to know' basis

Give them the materials and the skills they need 'right now', not those that they will need in twelve months time.

5. *Start by training whoever God has given you*

Sometimes leaders tell me, 'I don't have anyone to train.' I disagree. In a church plant setting God has always given us someone. However, sometimes they are not at the level of gifting or maturity that we hoped for. At these times we have to take whoever God has given us and be prepared to get our hands dirty by getting more involved in their lives and developing their leadership potential from wherever they are at.

The parable of the talents teaches us that as we use what God has given us, he will give us more. This applies just as much to training leaders as any other 'talent' he gives us. Conversely, if we squander what he has given us then we will lose what we already have.

As we train more leaders our capacity to minister to more people grows and our ability to make a difference increases. This begs the question, 'What can we believe God for?'

* * *

Faith is a critical element of the church planter's armoury and I will spend the next chapter outlining some of the most important lessons that we need to learn in this regard.

12

THE GIFT OF FAITH AND CHURCH PLANTING

> 'Now faith is being sure of what we hope for and certain of what we do not see ... without faith it is impossible to please God, because anyone who comes to him must believe that he exists and that he rewards those who earnestly seek him.'
>
> Hebrews 11:1,6

As I began to plan and pray about starting a church in central London, the size of the financial challenge we were facing started to crystallise. At the time when we moved, London was the most expensive place to live in the world. The costs of hall hire alone looked like it would be beyond us.

As I pressed on with preparations there were several occasions when people sought to dissuade me from making the move. 'David, are you sure this is wise?' was the gist of their comments. 'Is this really possible?'

Strangely, their comments did not seem to affect me. God had given me an unshakeable faith that I should press on and that he would provide.

A few months before we moved, a pastor approached me to tell me that there was a businessman in his church who had heard what we were doing and wanted to help us out. 'How much do you need?' was the pastor's question.

I was somewhat taken aback. I had never been asked that question before, but I mumbled something about needing £50,000 towards hall hire for our first year. 'Oh,' was his response. 'He was thinking of more than that! Could you use £100,000?'

I was speechless with amazement and full of thanks for what God had just done! It felt a bit like the opening of the Jordan for Joshua – an insuperable obstacle had suddenly become nothing because of God's intervention.

Faith is an essential element of our toolkit as church planters. You will often face difficult and apparently intractable situations. It is faith that will enable you to overcome these and move on with God.

Faith

Faith is foundational to the Christian life. Not only is it the basis of our salvation, but it is essential to live obediently every day as believers (2 Cor. 5:7).

However, when we respond to a specific call from the Lord to start a church, the faith challenges often increase significantly.

Here are a few examples:

1. *Faith for your own call*

When God calls us to be involved with church planting, one of the biggest battles we have is often with ourselves. 'Can I do this? Am I able to pull this off?' are the kind of questions that go through our head. This is nothing new. Gideon felt exactly the same when God called him to lead the people of God (Judg. 6:11–16).

However, if we allow such thoughts to go unhindered they will squeeze the life and faith out of us. It is very important that we learn to deal ruthlessly with such thinking and learn to think God's thoughts rather than our own.

2. Faith for your family

Church planting often requires change for the whole family. Usually it means our children face the challenges of moving home, making new friends and settling in a new school.

Our children need parents who will lead them with real faith. This will be a great blessing and a safeguard for them. Faith-filled parents are a great protection for their children from fear and discouragement.

As a result, we have to go through the process of coming to faith for our family and then helping our children to do the same.

3. Faith for the move

So often the sums do not add up when you are planning to move house to get a new church started.

This requires that you look to God to provide financially. This is often the first miracle that God works as a church plant prepares to start – providing the resources to get a leader moving.

'We bought our first home at the height of the house price boom in the 1980's. Five years later the house had fallen to half it's original price and we were in significant debt as a result.

We were sitting in our living room one day when the person who had been coaching us on our church plant said to us, "You know, if you are going to have any more children, then you need to move house".

At this, my wife laughed. "If you knew just how much debt we are in you would not suggest we thought about moving," was her response.

Quick as a flash, our coach came back at us: "If you can trust God for houses for the poor ... [which we had] ... then you can trust God for a house for yourself," he replied.

We knew this was God's word for us. It went right into our hearts and we began to pray.

The miracles followed and within six months we had moved house and cleared our debts entirely. God had taught us a massive lesson.

Never assume that something is impossible if it is God's will!'

David Stroud

4. *Faith for gathering a team*

One of the unique elements of church planting is that we are calling people 'to ourselves'. In the early days there is very little for people to join other than ourselves and our vision.

Consequently a leader must be deeply at ease with himself and confident that God has called him to say to someone, 'Come and join me.'

'God's work, done in God's way will never lack God's supplies.'[1]

Hudson Taylor

5. *Faith to overcome problems and obstacles we face*

One thing that we can be very sure of is that we will face unexpected challenges as we seek to develop the church plant and they can come in just about any shape or form. Our job as leaders is to develop ways of dealing with these challenges so that God's work can go forward.

Faith is fundamental to this because it fuels energy and creativity.

Israel's army became so intimidated by Goliath that they could not see a way through – they simply stayed in hiding and trembled every time Goliath challenged them to a fight. To my mind, it was David's faith that caused him to feel so outraged by Goliath's dominance. This then led to his creative approach to slaying giants. In turn, this act of faith coupled with action led to a great breakthrough for the whole army!

'One of the biggest faith tests for us came through "intimidation" before we moved. Several people offered to move with us, but backed out once they saw what Handsworth was like. Many people we met told us stories about being mugged and repeatedly burgled in the area. On one trip up our car mysteriously caught fire on the motorway, and on another trip, both Louise and I had very real suicidal thoughts for about half an hour. The house we were due to stay in turned out to be derelict and had previously been a drug den. When we went to see it a Police helicopter was hovering directly over it! The day before we moved in (to a different house!) someone tried to burgle our neighbours and the first morning we woke up in Birmingham, someone had been brutally murdered just around the corner.

Actually Handsworth has proved to be lovely — safe, very friendly and by far the happiest place we have ever lived. We have found it to be a great place to bring up our family.

My guess is that every church plant has its challenges. Actually moving here and "hammering our stake into the ground" was one of our hardest faith tests, but I believe that facing early obstacles forced us quickly to count the cost of living in an inner city and commit wholeheartedly for the long term. I often think that a lot of the blessing we have seen since stems from these early decisions.'

Martin White, The Crown Church, Birmingham

6. Faith to spot new opportunities as they appear

Opportunities often present themselves out of the blue. Sometimes the busyness of life means that we do not even look at them properly. We turn them down because we are already feeling stretched and over challenged.

This is where faith becomes a powerful weapon. Believing God will sometimes enable us to grasp opportunities that would otherwise slip through our fingers.

Faith helps us gain God's perspective on whatever is going on.

'It was not very long after we arrived in Manchester that God spoke to us really clearly, telling us that faith should characterise the way we moved forward as a church plant. This was reinforced by Colin Baron's encouragement to always have a faith goal in our annual budget (Colin was overseeing the church at the time).

As a result we took on an evangelist part time, although the church was not yet quite covering my costs. This was a massive stretch of faith for us, but it led to twenty-five responses to the gospel during the year.

A little later we were faced with the challenge of whether to move into the city centre. A good venue had become available on the university campus, but it required a 20% increase in our total budget to pay for it.

In faith we signed the contract and received a cheque for the first two months rent from a friend in another part of the country the following Monday. The move to the city centre has shaped our strategy and finances ever since.'

Howard Kellett, Hope Church, Manchester

How to keep faith fresh

1. Keep your devotional life strong

Faith comes from the Lord. It is as you connect with God, pray and read his word that fresh faith often comes. Make sure your times with the Lord do not get lost in the mountain of activity that church planting demands.

2. Get connected to other leaders who are full of faith

Like leadership, faith is more 'caught than taught'. I have often received faith for something in a moment as I have listened to someone else share with me what God has been doing in his or her life.

Make sure that you have some other leaders you connect with from time to time who strengthen you in this way.

3. Keep reading books that remind you of what God has done in the past

Stories of other church planters and those God has used to reach many for him can be a great tonic.

4. Remember that the words you speak also have a powerful effect on your levels of faith

This works both ways: positive words make one feel stronger, negative words sap energy and life (Prov. 16:24).

5. Keep praying for what God will do in the future and keep asking him to fulfil your vision

Don't just spend your time praying about your day to day needs, but keep lifting your eyes to the horizon and focus on the wonderful things that God wants to do in the long term.

* * *

It is exciting to think of the battles that you will win through exercising the faith that God will give you. However, there is another element to the winning of battles which is very important and that is the power of *prayer*. As a church planter you will need to be a 'pray-er'. You will also need to teach your church plant to pray as well. This is the subject to which we now turn.

13

PRAYER AND
CHURCH PLANTING

'Ask and it will be given to you; seek and you will find; knock
and the door will be opened to you. For everyone who asks
receives; he who seeks finds; and to him who knocks, the door
will be opened. Which of you, if his son asks for bread, will
give him a stone? Or if he asks for a fish, will give him a snake?
If you, then, though you are evil, know how to give good gifts
to your children, how much more will your Father in heaven give
good gifts to those who ask him!'

Matthew 7:7–11

'And pray in the Spirit on all occasions with all kinds of prayers
and requests. With this in mind, be alert and always keep on
praying for all the saints.'

Ephesians 6:18

'To be a Christian without prayer is no more possible than to be
alive without breathing.'

Martin Luther King Jr

'Prayer is a master weapon. We should be greatly wise if we
used it more and did so with more specific purpose.'[1]

C.H. Spurgeon

For a period of time in Birmingham I invited a small group of leaders to join me in prayer on a Sunday evening. We had some wonderful times seeking God together. These occasions were full of energy and the Holy Spirit. Sometimes God would speak to us prophetically for one another and at other times we would be directed to pray for particular areas of church life. Whatever we prayed for we would always finish those evenings confident that God was with us and believing him for greater blessing.

These evenings also really helped my leaders understand what was on my heart and what I was believing God for. I know they also helped keep them motivated and focused. I thank God too for the deep bond of love and camaraderie that developed as we prayed and served God together.

Prayer is one of the most powerful weapons that a church planter has. In this section we look at how you can use it personally to help the church to become an effective prayer powerhouse.

The role of prayer in church planting

Jesus taught his disciples to pray (Matt. 6:9–15) and modelled prayer in a way that clearly underlined its importance (Luke 6:12; Matt. 14:23).

This is all the more important in a pioneering situation where you are having to trust God for many miraculous breakthroughs.

Make sure that you ...

1. Pray personally

It is crucial that you are drawing on God's strength yourself by spending time with him in prayer.

'I was always convinced about the theological priority of prayer, but as an activist I wanted to have time to reach out to people beyond

our core group. I didn't realise at the time the impact a four day mission from Indian healing evangelist Ram Babu would have on my daily routine. He challenged me to rise early and pray in tongues an hour a day.

During those first three years I would pray and then set out to spend the morning in prayer up and down the streets of Hillingdon as I hand delivered leaflets to almost a quarter of a million houses. It was a great way of leaning on the sovereignty of God whilst taking personal responsibility for the mission he had given me. During that time we only had four Sundays without a first time visitor and we saw some powerful healings.'

Pete Cornford, Crown Church, Hillingdon

It is always a challenge to spend time praying, but this can be particularly pressurised at a time when there are so many other demands on your time. Nevertheless, resist the temptation to cut prayer out with the promise to return to it when things quiet down.

Remember that prayer is actually the best way for a leader to use his time.

'I feel like a businessman who perceives that a certain line of goods pays better than any other in his store, and who purposes making it his chief investment; who, in fact sees an inexhaustible supply and an almost unlimited demand for a profitable article and intends to go in for it more than for anything else. The demand is the lost state of these tens of thousands of Lisu and Kachin – their ignorance, their superstition, their sinfulness; their bodies, their minds, their souls; the supply is the grace of God to meet this need – to be brought down to them by the persevering prayers of a considerable company of God's people. All I want to do is, as a kind of middleman, to bring the supply and the demand together.'[2]

James Fraser, missionary to the Lisu Tribe, China

2. *Pray with your leaders*

As a group of leaders start to emerge in the church it is also important to spend time together praying with them.

This can prove to be a great environment in which to share what is on your heart in a more candid way than might be possible when the whole church plant is gathered together.

You will often find that as you pray together as leaders, God will encourage you and speak to you about issues in the church. Praying together also binds you together more deeply and helps you clarify and refine the vision as you call out to God together.

3. *Pray with the church*

Prayer should be one of the distinguishing features of the life of the church. Jesus summed this up by saying that the church should be a 'house of prayer' (Matt. 21:13).

I have found it very beneficial to have regular times of prayer when the church can gather together and seek God for his blessing and his direction.

Apart from the obvious blessing of being able to pray together, there are a number of other benefits that come from regular prayer times. These include:

- Being able to model to others *how to pray*. Every Christian knows they should pray, but most struggle to pray as much as they would like. One of the main reasons for this is that they simply do not know what to say or how to keep going. Times of corporate prayer can provide a wonderful opportunity for them to start to learn how to pray with faith and passion, trusting God for a breakthrough.

- *Hearing God together*. As the church prays, God will often speak through prophetic words. There are times when these powerfully catch men and women's hearts and deeply affect the identity of the church.

There are other occasions when you can introduce prophetic words that have been brought to you for the whole church and pray into them together.

'Probably the most significant prophetic word that we received as a church plant came during a time of prayer in a leader's prayer meeting. David Devenish came to me with a prophetic word for the church. He said that he could see us doing a huge triple jump, that each leap was different from the one before and that each one required faith, but that put together they would enable us to make great progress as a church.

As he spoke, I felt deep in my spirit that he was referring to moving from one venue to another and I began to wonder whether we would move, fairly quickly from one place to the next. This was exactly how it turned out.

We worshipped in Covent Garden for the first year before taking a great "leap" over the river (to a wine museum!) and then back into the West End to meet in a theatre just off Piccadilly Circus. Each step was an absolutely massive challenge for us, but led to enormous blessing.

We often referred to this prophetic word and prayed together about it. Unless God had spoken to us in this way, I do not think we would have had the courage that we needed to complete the triple jump.'

David Stroud

- *People grow in their ownership of future events.* When people start to pray together for future church events they often come away with a much greater sense of ownership than they had before. God births

something in prayer that remains after the praying is
finished. .

- *People grow in their ownership of the vision.* It is often
  during times of prayer that people catch a burden
  for the people you are trying to reach and the sort of
  church that God has called you to build.

- Prayer times are great opportunities to *share the
  vision that God has given you* and to pray into it as a
  church together.

We have now looked at the preparatory work that is
required before a church plant is started and the qualities
that God is looking for in those who will lead these church
plants. This has now cleared the ground for the biggest
question of all: what are the key ingredients for actually
getting a church plant started?

Section 3:
The planting phase

14

APOSTLES, PROPHETS AND CHURCH PLANTING

'It was he who gave some to be apostles, some to be prophets, some to be evangelists, and some to be pastors and teachers, to prepare God's people for works of service, so that the body of Christ may be built up until we all reach unity in the faith and in the knowledge of the Son of God and become mature, attaining to the whole measure of the fullness of Christ.'

Ephesians 4:11–13

'By the grace God has given me, I laid a foundation as an expert builder.'

1 Corinthians 3:10

'What was the work of an apostle? Surely he was pre-eminently a church founder, a wise master builder who laid foundations.'[1]

Terry Virgo

I am profoundly grateful for the people that God has put in my life as apostles whilst I have given my time to planting churches. It has been of enormous personal benefit. The presence of these men in my life has made me bigger; their advice and counsel has often helped me live better; their partnership has made me stronger. I know that as a result of these relationships I have lived with a much broader outlook than I would have done otherwise. The world has become a bigger place, the importance of essential doctrines has become so much clearer to me and I have known that my endeavours have been caught up in a greater purpose.

These men have advised and encouraged me as I have made my plans and pushed forward. They have helped me appoint elders and, on occasion, have advised on disagreements or problems that have arisen within the team. They have saved churches that I have led from significant heartbreak by their counsel and direction.

In short, apostolic ministry has proved to be fundamental to my efforts to plant churches.

This is just as it should be and is part of the great benefit of apostolic ministry for the church planter. All church planters should experience the blessing of working under the umbrella of apostolic ministry in this way.

In order to look at the practical benefits of apostolic ministry more closely, we need to take a step back and consider where authority lies in a church plant.

Where does authority lie in a church planting situation?

If a group of people are going to work well together at any level they need to be able to identify how decisions are made and who carries authority. This is no different in the church than in other arenas of life.

In New Testament times, God-given authority rested with the team of elders based in each church (it is interesting to note that you never come across a single elder leading a church in Scripture). This authority was exercised

by the loving, sacrificial, servant leadership of those God
had appointed (1 Pet. 5:1–4; Acts 20:28).

Prior to elders being set in place, authority came from
the apostle and his team who were planting the church.
It was they who would then appoint the elders in due
course.

> 'Paul and Barnabas appointed elders for them in each church
> and, with prayer and fasting, committed them to the Lord, in
> whom they had put their trust.'
>
> Acts 14:23

In the same way, it is important that as church plants are
started we recognise that the God-given authority rests
with the apostolic team until elders are appointed. This
means that the church plant leader is not left by himself,
but leads in liaison with the apostolic team and it is clear
that final authority rests with them.

Once elders have been appointed the dynamic changes.
The elders become responsible for the life of the church and
apostolic ministry serves the church as they are invited to
by the local eldership.

Coaching and apostolic ministry

We encourage every church planter to ensure they have
a coach who can assist them during the church planting
process.

A coach is someone who has planted a church himself
and has accumulated wisdom in church planting matters.
He represents the apostolic team and will help the church
planter with the pragmatic challenges and issues that arise
as a church plant goes forward.

The coach may well also provide other elements of support that you would expect to get from apostolic ministry, especially as he will be working on behalf of the apostolic team. However, do not expect any one person to give you everything you need in terms of input and advice. God has created different ministries because they have differing contributions to make and we are likely to need them all at different times as we grow and progress.

What should you expect from your involvement with an apostolic team?

1. *A genuine relational connection with the apostolic team*

When you read the letters that Paul wrote to the churches he cared for, you get the feel of genuine, loving relationships (e.g. Rom. 16). There is no sense of hierarchy and institutionalism here, but of people who are genuinely connected with each other and sharing a common sense of mission together to extend God's kingdom.

This 'relational' element is pivotal to apostolic ministry working well.

This does not necessarily mean that every church planter will be close to an apostle personally.

Certainly, Paul often expressed a longing to be with churches that he had not been able to get to (Rom. 1:11–13; 1 Thess. 2:17–18). He was also aware that there were times when a spiritual battle raged over his travel plans.

As a result, he sometimes sent others on his behalf. Timothy went to the Corinthians (1 Cor. 4:17) and it seems that Epaphras started the church in Colossae (Col. 1:7; Col. 4:12). These men functioned on Paul's behalf and often with his authority.

Many of the same dynamics function today. Apostles cannot be everywhere they would like to be and will often send members of their teams on their behalf to represent them and minister to churches on their behalf.

2. Support and care to you and the church plant

This relationship provides a natural connection point to turn to when support is needed.

It also provides an important connection point when problems or challenges arise in the church. It can be enormously helpful for you and the church to have someone who the church knows who can help them through a challenging season.

3. A team that will assist in the laying of doctrinal foundations in the life of the church (1 Cor. 3:10–11; Heb. 6:1)

This manual has not spent a lot of time focusing on the importance of doctrine, but it is, of course, vital that every church is clear on what it believes and that the church is living with the powerful reality of these truths in their lives.

These doctrines function as foundations to the life of the church, ensuring that it grows strong and tall.

One of the features of apostolic ministry is that it has a particular ability to lay these foundations in the life of the church and you can expect their assistance, where necessary, in helping you to do this.

4. A team with a diverse array of gifts that can help equip the church in different dimensions of Christian ministry, including prophetically and evangelistically (Eph. 4:11–12)

The ministries mentioned in Ephesians 4 bring a broad array of ministry to the local church.

5. *A team that gives the church plant a broader vision than simply their own mission field (2 Cor. 10:15-16)*

It is really important for a church plant to be focused on its local mission, but this can also, ironically, become a limiting factor if you are not careful. One of the real benefits of working with an apostolic team is that through their teaching and the stories of their travels they remind you that there is a bigger world out there that is on God's heart.

The team will also provide ways in which your people can be involved in contributing to that mission and become connected to other like minded churches.

'For my first church plant, it took a long time to develop a leadership team. Receiving coaching and apostolic oversight provided much needed security for the church, as well as keeping me going personally. They really helped the church push forward and were the key for some of the breakthroughs we had in St Ives. Tony Thompson helped us lay great apostolic foundations and got us looking outwards. Prophets brought breakthroughs in vision and faith and an experienced pastor helped us solve some tricky pastoral situations.

Oversight has always been a blessing and one of my most important diary commitments. I believe Apostles as well as Prophets bring a reward (Matt. 10:41) in faith and clarity that moves the church plant forward. I would invite Tony to ask questions or make comments on any area of church, so I approached those coaching times with nervousness at times, but always came away excited, encouraged, envisioned and often challenged.

When elders were appointed our relationship with the apostolic team remained open and strong.

Working with an apostolic team also opened our eyes to world mission. Tony Thompson took me with him to a church plant in Niger, West Africa, and this resulted in the church starting to support them in prayer and financially.'

Andy Moyle, Gateway Church, King's Lynn

6. A team that will assist you in appointing of elders (Acts 14:23)

Apostolic ministry can be enormously helpful in assessing the suitability of men for eldership in the local church. The fact that they come from outside the local situation enables a more objective perspective and brings insights that could otherwise be missed.

7. A team that provokes and reminds you and the church plant to remember the poor (Gal. 2:10)

To find ways of caring for the poor and expressing God's mercy can be costly and sacrificial, but it also often leads to wonderful times of God's blessing and miraculous breakthrough.

Apostolic ministry will remind us of the priority of the poor in God's heart and provoke and equip us to reach out to them as well.

The appointing of elders

1. The appointing of elders is an important point in the growth of any church and is particularly important for a church plant (Titus 1:5)

It demonstrates the church is 'growing up' and has enough mature leadership to stand on its own feet.

2. Apostolic ministry and their delegates will play a significant role in this process

They will assist the church plant leader in identifying prospective elders. They may also help train and develop them to the point where they can be released into their new role. Their appointment will involve hands being laid upon them by those who have been overseeing the church plant to this point (Acts 14:23).

3. *It is important not to rush this process (1 Tim. 5:22)*

If necessary one can appoint a leadership team in the interim before an eldership is established. This has the benefit of enabling prospective elders to 'grow into' their role and it gives the church an opportunity to respond to their leadership and feel secure with the team.

The sending church and the church plant

To have a strong local church involved in the planting of a new church can be an enormous help and this can often happen when the plant is close to the established church.

The existing church can provide:

- A strong and experienced team that already know each other and have a clear understanding of the sort of church that they want to build.
- Resources that the church plant do not have at their disposal: specialist care ministries, experience and advice on difficult pastoral situations, youth work, etc.
- Additional Sunday meeting manpower in the early days: worship leaders, preachers, even 'rent-a-crowd'.
- Money.
- Prayer support.

However it is important to bear in mind that:

1. *This does not mean that the leader of the sending church should automatically take oversight of the new church plant*

This is a very different role that requires a different set of gifts from leading a church. Therefore it is important for the local church eldership to look for the advice and direction of the apostolic team as plans for the church plant start to develop.

2. *The apostolic team will also help bring direction in terms of when the 'umbilical cord' should be cut between the existing church and the church plant*

This ensures that the church plant gains the independence that it needs.

This is an important decision. If the cord is cut prematurely it can result in a weak 'baby' plant. Equally, if it is delayed too long it can result in both churches suffering damage.

'I have twice left strong church bases to plant a new church in a nearby town.

On both occasions there have been challenges and tensions as we have sought to judge how to pace the separating process. Strong relationships have helped us through as we have looked at issues such as when the established church should stop paying salaries and when the church plant should start their own prayer meetings!

However, for me the most unexpected issues arose as I was leaving St Neots to plant a church in Luton. I had handed over the leadership, but my house move was delayed and so I was still living in St Neots, giving my time to the new plant. What I was unaware of was that my continued presence working from the church offices was preventing the new team taking things forward and creating their own identity. I was asked to leave and work from home! My initial reaction was total surprise and bewilderment. But I quickly understood and was pleased they felt able to ask, realising that greater tension and possibly damage could have arisen otherwise. However, it didn't prevent just a few moments when other thoughts dominated!'

Tony Thompson, Hope Church, Luton

When does a church plant become a church?

In the New Testament there is no clear demarcation between a church plant and a church, so the question of when a church plant becomes a church does not arise!

However, as a family of churches, we have found it helpful to be able to acknowledge a time when a church plant has 'grown up' and is clearly recognised as a church in its own right.

The characteristics we are currently looking for are:

1. *That a clear community has been established. Amongst other things this will include:*

   • Clear leadership (which will exercise, amongst other things, church discipline)
   • Church membership
   • Baptism and communion

2. *That there is a plurality of leadership. Nowhere in the New Testament do we find a church with only one leader*

We should therefore always be looking for a leadership team or eldership in the local setting.

However, even before a local team is recognised there will still be a plurality of leadership in place due to the fact that the apostolic team are working together with the church plant leader.

Whilst in practical terms the church plant leader will take many of the day to day decisions, he will involve other members of the apostolic team in the key decisions until he has an eldership team working with him in the church.

As long as this dynamic of shared leadership is in place and one can see a leadership team starting to emerge, then we see no reason to delay in recognising the community as a church.

3. *That the church plant is strong enough to show that it will be around for the long term*

This may include any number of factors, but will include a critical mass of people (the actual number of people might vary from setting to setting) and the ability to be financially self-supporting.

4. *That the apostolic team overseeing the church plant are happy for the church plant to be recognised as a fully-fledged church.*

It is important to have a good understanding of the role of apostles and prophets, but it is even better to have a good experience of them. Make sure you do not go church planting without being connected with these key ministries!

* * *

We can now turn to the very heart of the process of church planting: what do you actually do to get the church plant up and running?

15

GETTING TO THE LAUNCH 1: TWO DIFFERENT MODELS

'He [Paul] took the disciples with him and had discussions daily in the lecture hall of Tyrannus. This went on for two years, so that all the Jews and Greeks who lived in the province of Asia heard the word of the Lord.'

Acts 19:9–10

Our first meeting for Oasis Church, Birmingham, was on the first Wednesday evening in January 1999 in our living room. As we talked and prayed together that evening there was one question no one asked but everyone was thinking: 'Is this going to work? Are we going to be able to get a church started?'

After nine busy months we were a lot closer to answering that question as we prepared to take the leap to weekly Sunday meetings.

I turned up on that first Sunday morning with a sense of excitement and nervousness. How would it go? Who would come along? Would we get the sort of power-off from the ground that we were hoping for?

I had no reason to worry. All our regulars turned up, of course, but also a whole pile of other people as well who had heard about the church starting, some of whom seemed to have already decided to get involved.

The worship was full of the presence of God, people responded really well to the preaching and we enjoyed some really good fellowship over tea and coffee at the end. The seventeen people who had been in our living room in the January became eighty people meeting regularly that autumn. Oasis Church, Birmingham, had been born. The initial group that met in my living room had, under God's grace, done just what they had dreamed of doing: they had taken a church from conception to the point of being born.

In this section we will look at how we go through the process of getting to the point of starting a Sunday meeting. Broadly speaking there are two different models to consider.

Model 1: From the Ground Up

Building from the ground up requires that you gather people in small groups before starting a weekly Sunday meeting.

The goal, ideally, is to gather enough people in small groups so that when you start on a Sunday you have the same number of people attending as an average sized church in your area.

Although for onlookers it seems that the church has suddenly come out of nowhere, there is a tangible sense of love and shared vision which clearly communicates that this is something rather more substantial than simply a crowd who has turned up to see what this new church is like.

Model 2: From the Top Down

Starting from the 'top down' means that you begin the church with a large team that can sustain weekly Sunday meetings from the outset of the church plant.

This approach relies a lot on drawing a good number of newcomers to meetings quickly and then turning the crowd that gathers into a church. This is done as values are taught, small groups are formed and vision is cast.

Something of a hybrid model can happen when an existing church decides to plant a new church close to where it is located. Those who are going to be part of the church plant have often already formed small groups and begun to draw together around a clear vision, even before they leave the mother church. Then, on a planned date, a number of members start meeting in a new location as a church plant.

Both approaches have advantages and disadvantages. We'll look at both of them in more detail:

Advantages of building from the ground up

1. *You have an opportunity to connect with everyone as they join the church*

As you gather people into small groups and host social events you find that everyone in the church has been to your house at some point and many have eaten with you or at least had a chance to chat with you in a social setting.

This is a great way of sending out the message that church is all about relationships.

Even more importantly, you have a chance to build the church one by one. The early core are all won to you personally. People get to know you and trust you. They start to give their hearts to you. This breeds trust and loyalty which will prove to be a great foundation for the future.

2. *The small groups become central to the life of the church*

These are the only meetings that are available to attend, so their importance is underscored. Churches who start in this way tend to find there is a higher attendance of small groups even after the church planting phase, because people understand that they are central to everything that is happening.

You also have a great opportunity to build a common genetic code into the groups. Rather than the groups all behaving differently (according to the leader's previous experience), you have an opportunity to model small group life and multiply groups that function in the same way.

3. *This model can fit well with the church planter being in secular employment*

This model does not require time availability during the day and does not require lots of money.

4. *It also particularly suits those leaders who have strong relational skills and enjoy meeting people and building new relationships.*

'When we began the church plant in Chichester we started weekly Sunday morning meetings well before we launched the church publicly.

We met in a village hall which was deliberately chosen for being a few miles outside of the city we were planting into.

This really helped people to feel like we were a church and not just a "midweek group", but did not pressure us to deliver a full blown public Sunday meeting before we were ready. Each week we clearly stated that we were an embryonic church working towards a full Sunday meeting, but that this was not it yet. Visitors, far from being put off, were excited at the chance to be involved in helping towards launching something new. This phase was a key time for numerical and relational growth.

We launched publicly when we had a venue that would work for us in the right location, enough resources to sustain worship of a reasonable musical standard, good enough preaching, an excellent welcome, and a way of looking after the children well. To put it another way, we went public when we had created something together that we were happy to invite our friends to.'

Steve Petch, Grace Church, Chichester

Disadvantages of building from the ground up

1. *Some people will be reluctant to come to church in a home*

Some people will expect a 'normal' church to meet in a public building and are suspicious about entering a home for a meeting of this sort. Moreover, the fact that you are not meeting on a Sunday only compounds this problem and makes some people reluctant to join.

The best approach with people like this is simply to be patient and stay in touch with them. Some of them will join you once you have started regular meetings on a Sunday. In the meantime, there will be others who are happy to join you during this 'underground' phase. You just have to meet enough people to find them.

2. *Young families become concerned that their children (who are too young to come to a midweek small group) are not going anywhere to church*

It is important to be sympathetic to this concern.

Some families will continue to attend another nearby church on Sundays during the gathering phase for the sake of their children, whilst remaining clear that their loyalties are with the church plant.

'In Birmingham we had a number of families who were concerned that their children might feel that they had stopped going to church and were backsliding (this was rather ironic, given the fact that they *were actually highly committed to a risk taking, pioneering church plant!)*

As a result, the families organised their own get together every other Sunday morning in one of their homes. It was deliberately very informal and it was very clear that this was, in no way, a Sunday church meeting, but an opportunity for the children to be together. One or two of the parents would teach a Bible story and there would be a short time of prayer and lots of time to play. In this way, the children were getting some input and were understanding that they were part of something, but the church was not being forced to start a Sunday meeting prematurely.'

David Stroud

3. *It is possible to get stuck in this process if you are not a strong gatherer*

When this happens the church plant often goes to a Sunday morning meeting in the hope that others will come as a result. However, starting a Sunday meeting in and of itself does not solve anything.

In fact, it can create a fresh set of challenges, because sustaining a Sunday meeting requires lots of people to work very hard, setting up, caring for the children, organising refreshments, running the PA, and so on. If new people do not start to come along immediately, then after a while people will become tired and de-motivated as more and more energy is required just to keep things going.

Advantages of launching from the top down

1. *You have a church meeting on day one*

This is easier for those who have been in full time ministry as it is more familiar ground. It tends to work best if you are a strong preacher, because it means people are immediately benefiting from one of your strongest gifts. It can also be an easier way to start a church if you are not so natural at building new relationships.

2. *The new church immediately has legitimacy*

It is meeting on a Sunday in a public space. This is what people expect when they get invited to a new church. Some people find it easier to join as a result.

Disadvantages of the Top Down approach

1. *It is easy to shortcut the preparation for the launch*

The team need to really understand what you are trying to do, what you are expecting from them and how the whole Sunday event will hang together. This is a lot easier if most of the team are from an existing church and know each other, but even so, you will need to take some time to spell out what is going to happen, especially highlighting the ways in which it may be different from the church many have come from.

2. *It is easy to forget that planting a church is all about people!*

Whether you start with small groups or a crowd you have to get among people, get to know them, share your heart with them and communicate your love and care for them.

In the busyness of making Sunday church happen this can easily be forgotten, especially for those who naturally lean towards being in front of a crowd and preaching rather than pastoring and caring for people.

If you fall into this category be careful! Do not let busyness, preparation and organisation steal all your time. You need to be with people.

*'Even if your preaching is not quite as good as you could make it and your organisation not quite as polished as you would like it to be, remember that your first priority is always **people**, and especially people you have not met before.'*

Tony Thompson, Hope Church, Luton

3. *You have no small group infrastructure in place to gather people into*

As a result, you will need to start small groups at the same time as you start Sunday meetings.

If you leave it until later it may be hard to get small groups to 'take' and be regarded as an essential part of the life of the church.

4. *You will have a lot to communicate*

You will not be able to take anything for granted in terms of people's common understanding of the Christian life. Therefore you will have to ensure that you are stating over and over what is most important to you about the Christian life and the church.

5. *This approach is more expensive*

It requires that you hire a hall, own a PA and children's equipment, etc. You may also need to be working for the church at least part time very quickly. All of these things mean that you will need to raise some money before you start and ensure that you do some careful planning and budgeting over the early months.

6. It is a high-risk strategy

If no one turns up in the first few weeks then things can become very hard work if you don't have enough people to make everything happen.

If this continues for a protracted period of time you should discuss seriously with your coach what your next step should be. In larger urban areas you can consider stopping the church, relocating its epicentre and starting again at a later date or with a different strategy.

'I didn't want to start with two or three people pottering around in a front room. It just didn't feel like what was in my heart to start with. So that's why we set a year to gather, because I felt that God had called us to plant with a team of fifty. I wanted to major on our Sunday mornings and Alpha, the two big things that had really captured my heart which would lead to building a big city church and winning the lost.

Being part of Newfrontiers made all the difference. We felt like we were being launched from a well-resourced, big, capable group of friends and we didn't ever feel lost, isolated, or lacking in faith as we faced challenges. We had money in the bank that enabled us to do the things we felt were relevant to our city centre context. But it wasn't automatic. My wife Jo and I were regularly praying for leaders, musicians, families and students to join us before we launched.'

Chris and Jo Kilby, Life Church, Southampton

As you pray and talk with your coach about the best model to adopt in your situation, remember that there are a number of other key elements to getting through to the launch in good shape. It is these factors that we consider next.

16

GETTING TO THE LAUNCH 2: GATHERING AND MULTIPLYING SMALL GROUPS

'On the Sabbath we [Paul and Silas] went outside the city gate to the river, where we expected to find a place of prayer. We sat down and began to speak to the women who had gathered there. One of those listening was a woman named Lydia, a dealer in purple cloth from the city of Thyatira, who was a worshiper of God. The Lord opened her heart to respond to Paul's message. When she and the members of her household were baptised, she invited us to her home. "If you consider me a believer in the Lord," she said, "come and stay at my house." And she persuaded us.'

Acts 16:13–15

At the start of the New Year I sat in my new home in Birmingham with my fellow leader, Adrian Hurst, and we started to talk about what we needed to do to plant a church.

We made a long list of things that we should focus on. Many of them were very practical. We needed to get a telephone line installed in my house so that people could get in touch with us easily and we needed some stationery supplies. We knew that we should start work on forming a new charitable trust and a whole host of other things.

However, good as all these things were, we realised there was only one thing that was essential; there was one thing that would probably, in the end, cause our church plant to stand or fall. That was our ability to meet people we did not know and draw them into the church.

In this section we will look at how you go about this process of meeting people and gathering them into a community.

Gathering

A quick word about the term 'gathering'. As you start to draw people into the life of the church, you will find that they are at differing stages on their spiritual journey. Some will clearly be non-Christians who need evangelising. However, there will be many others who you meet who will be interested in the new church and do not fall into this category. They will include people who have been away from God for a long time, other Christians who have not been going to church for a while and want to get involved again, and Christians moving into the area looking for a new church.

I am using the term 'gathering' to describe your building relationships with all these different types of people as you seek to draw them into the church plant.

How does the gathering process work?

1. *Have a plan for how you are going to reach people before you start the plant*

This should consist of at least five different ways in which you will meet people. Some of these approaches will work better than others, which is why you are best to start with a number of options. It is hard to predict ahead of time precisely what will be effective and what will not.

Your coach should be asking you about this prior to you starting the church. Push yourself to come up with a number of ways in which you plan to meet people. Getting going with only one or two planned approaches leaves you very vulnerable if neither of them work.

2. During this period you need to be meeting as many people as possible

You should be hosting lots of parties, social events, picnics and anything else that you think your team will invite their friends to.

I have often asked people, 'If we organise such and such event would you be able to invite your unbelieving friends, as long as we promise not to talk about Jesus?!' Most people say 'yes' and bring people along.

I have found that our guests will always work out, somewhere along the line, that we are starting a church, but bringing them into a fun environment with laughing, smiling people is a much more effective way of drawing them in than trying prematurely to share the gospel with them.

3. Gathering men and women into the church plant is your number one priority at this stage

Be careful that you do not delegate this responsibility to others.

In the early days of the church plant people will stick with you for only two reasons:

- *Because of you*, if they decide they like you and could be led by you.

- *Because of your vision*. Some people will 'get' your vision and want to help you bring it into reality.

Don't ask for commitment to the church plant too early. My experience is that those who swear undying allegiance on their first contact with you do not normally stay around for very long!

I have always enjoyed watching people 'buy in' to what we are doing. It is rarely immediate, but happens over a period of time. It is important not to rush this process, but to let it happen naturally. Once they have bought in at a heart level to what you are doing, people will be ready to express their commitment.

'Pip and I arrived in Leeds with a small child and one more on the way. That was the extent of our church planting team. We knew it was going to take a lot of effort, but once we had settled in and got to know the city, we went people crazy!

We did everything we could to meet new people. If we went to a restaurant and saw someone sitting on their own, we would literally go over to their table and say, "Would you mind coming and sitting with us and being our friend? We don't know anyone in Leeds."

Everywhere we went we worked hard at being hyper-relational and during that year we gathered about 20–25 people who wanted to be our friends and come over on a Friday afternoon and dream about starting a new church.'

Matt and Pip Hatch, Mosaic Church, Leeds

4. *Remember to keep meeting new people*

In the early days, one of the things you are looking for are those who are ready to join you, but as yet do not know you exist. To find these people may mean meeting ten to twenty times that number!

Do not get so stuck into a few relationships at this point in time that you cannot keep finding and meeting new people.

> 'Most people work too hard on too few people.'
>
> John Wimber
> founder, Vineyard Christian Fellowships

5. It can be very easy to find that all your time is taken up with caring for those you already have once you have gathered thirty or so people

At this point in time, therefore, it is important to divide your time in half and give half of it to those you have gathered and half to meeting and drawing in new people.

> 'We had a well known Asian healing evangelist come when we were only fifty people. This meant us all giving generously, praying passionately and taking time off to help. We were thrown together with a big project that helped develop community as well as reaching out.
>
> When we had seventy-five people we held a community fun day (with donkey rides, three bouncy castles, a bird display, the local Fire Brigade, marching RAF etc) and we had 1,500 guests turn up! Community was extended as we planned, sweated and reflected, and we made lots of new contacts.'
>
> **Pete Cornford, The Crown Church, London**

Starting small groups

1. Be clear on what you want from your small groups and how they will fit into the overall church architecture once the church is up and running

Remember that the way in which you conduct your first small group will get reproduced many times over in the coming years as other groups are multiplied out of it. It is therefore important to be clear on how you want to do small group life before you start.

If you have not been involved in overseeing a small group system before then this is worth discussing with your coach.

2. *Start your first small group and continually seek to gather new people into the embryonic community*

3. *Constantly keep your eye out for potential leaders*

These will be able people who are buying into what you are doing, who have time available to give and are teachable. You need to be spending time with these people so that you can start to train them.

4. *Look to multiply groups*

If you do not have leaders ready you can always lead different groups on different nights yourself.

'When we started the King's Arms we were short of leaders we could ask to lead our small groups, so Philippa and I led the first three groups ourselves. This enabled us to keep multiplying groups. If we had not been prepared to lead groups on Tuesday, Wednesday and Thursday evenings then the plant would have grown much more slowly in those early days.

However, after a while we ran into a further challenge. No one else wanted to start a group. The trainee leaders told us that they were convinced that everyone would want to go to a group that the Strouds were leading. So Philippa and I handed over the leadership of all the groups we were leading and released further leaders to start two new groups. Suddenly we had five groups in place and we moved into coaching the leaders of those groups.'

David Stroud

5. *Once you have more than one group you need to consider when you are going to gather the groups together*

This needs to be done regularly so that people can meet others who are joining the church and so that you can bring teaching and direction to everyone in the church plant.

6. *Once you have a critical mass of people you can launch on a Sunday morning*

Multiplying small groups

1. *Make sure that you have a critical mass before going to two groups*

This means having at least twelve people attending (depending on the small group model you are using). Bear in mind the strength of the individuals who are coming along, not just the numbers. It is important that both groups have some of these stronger people as they will make a significant difference to the success of each new group.

2. *Identify the leader*

This could be you or it could be someone else – ideally someone who has led before.

3. *Tell the group a few weeks ahead of time that you will be multiplying on a specific date*

Make sure that your last time together has a celebratory feel. Find ways of reflecting on what God has done and how good he has been. For instance, you can ask people to share how life in the group has helped them, what has changed in their lives, etc.

4. *Provide support for the new leader*

Support should involve regular contact with the leader and helping them with any problems or challenges they are facing in the group. You will also need to help the leader think through how and when they will multiply their group.

One of the most effective ways of coaching a group is to go and visit it from time to time. However, do not feel that you have to play a very vocal, up front role. If you do, you will probably learn little about how the group normally runs when you are not there. It may be of greater worth to simply observe quietly for the evening.

Gathering the groups together and going to a weekly Sunday meeting

Once you have more than one group you will need to bring everyone together regularly for worship, teaching and to give an opportunity for people to be together. However, it is very important that this is not confused with the weekly Sunday meeting that is still to come.

In the meantime, either find another time of the week to draw everyone together or do something to make it clear that your gatherings are quite distinct from what is to come.

Here are a number of advantages of taking this approach:

1. *Moving to a Sunday meeting at the right time adds momentum to the church plant*

It is like benefiting from a rocket booster. Suddenly everything is fresh, new and exciting and it feels as if the church has suddenly taken a big leap closer to its goals.

The more distinct this change is from previous meetings, the greater the benefit you are likely to get.

2. *People have certain expectations of a normal church service*

People will expect good worship, good teaching and good quality children's work. These all take time to prepare during the week.

If you feel a pressure to provide these things, as if you were already a fully fledged church, then it will distract you and your team from the main purpose at this point: meeting new people.

3. *It will be hard to attract new people*

If you go to a weekly meeting too early then it will look and feel premature. You will simply not have the resources early on to provide the different components that others will be looking for when they visit.

'When we started in London we avoided these pitfalls by doing a number of things which made it really clear that we were not yet ready for "proper" church. We had no printed literature (including no weekly bulletin), no worship band (just someone playing an acoustic guitar), no children's work (there was a room that parents could take their children out to if they wanted) and we only met altogether every second Sunday. We explained each time we met that we were still in the process of getting ready for our launch and told everyone when we were planning to do that. This built a real sense of anticipation and excitement as we neared our launch date.'

David Stroud

Evangelism

One of the big goals for any church plant is to reach many unbelievers and see them come to Christ. It is therefore very important to start with a focus on those who do not know Christ.

However, do not put yourself under too much pressure to see people come to Christ right away. Personal evangelism is a process that includes sowing and reaping. Sometimes you can reap where other people have already done the hard work, but otherwise you have to be patient whilst God superintends this whole process from planting the seed in men and women's hearts to the point where they receive Christ.

Here's some pointers to bear in mind along the way:

1. The most effective form of evangelism in the UK at present is normal friendship evangelism

This is where Christians develop genuine friendships with unbelievers. Once these friendships have been established they will find opportunities to share their faith and invite their friends to an event at church, such as a special evangelistic meeting or an Alpha dinner.

2. If a church plant is going to become effective in evangelism it is important that those in leadership model this and lead by example

'When we started the church in Birmingham, Philippa and I both threw ourselves into the life of the wider community with the aim of finding those who were open to Christ. Amongst other things, Philippa became a governor at our children's school and I started a Neighbourhood Watch scheme on our road.

Neither of us saw fruit from these activities for some time, but getting involved was very good for both of us. It was also a powerful message to the rest of the team that we were serious about getting to know non-church goers and reaching them with the gospel.'

David Stroud

3. Some church members find they have plenty of opportunity to build relationships with unbelievers at work

If they have young children they will also find there are many opportunities to meet other parents through playgroups, inviting children over to play and other activities.

However, others need to be encouraged to find ways of meeting people. One of the most effective ways of doing this is for people to join community groups, sports teams or get involved in other activities that they really enjoy and also give them opportunities for friendship evangelism.

It is important that this is seen as a valuable way of spending time, as much as other church activities, otherwise prayer meetings, small group meetings and other church events take over and preclude the church from ever spending time with those that they want to reach.

'During the gathering process the number of church meetings needs to be kept as light as possible to enable friendship evangelism to flourish.'

Pete Cornford, The Crown Church, London

4. Once people have started to engage with those who do not know Christ and build relationships with them, they will need further training on sharing the gospel

Events will also need to be put on (or Alpha courses started) so that they have things to invite their friends to.

* * *

As you give yourself to reaching out to others you can expect the church plant to begin to grow. The big call ahead is when to start your weekly Sunday meetings and how to gain the most from the launch event. We look at this more closely in the next chapter.

17

YOU ONLY LAUNCH ONCE: STARTING WEEKLY SUNDAY MORNING MEETINGS

'You really only get one shot at the first public service. In other words, if it doesn't go well, if you're unprepared, it's not like you can re-load and try again next week. People who come will pretty much make up their mind if they want to make a second visit based on that first week. You want to really make sure you're ready to pull it off in such a way that people will want to come back. (Translation: Good worship, good preaching, excellent childcare.) Otherwise you're back to having a small core of people, very few return visitors and an uphill road to try and gather people again.'[1]

Jeff Bailey and Steve Nicholson,
Vineyard Coaches and Church Planters Manual

'Don't be afraid to take a big step when one is indicated. You can't cross a chasm in two small steps.'

David Lloyd George

The memory of 'launch day' for each of the churches that we have planted is seared on my memory. On each occasion it was a day of intense excitement and energy. We had changed jobs, moved homes and worked like crazy for some months and it was all about to happen.

On each occasion it was a defining day for the future of the church.

The build up starts as you visualise in your mind's eye exactly how you want your Sunday meetings to work, what you need your team members to be doing and what a massively successful launch would look like.

Then you form a plan to make it happen. You find a venue, ensure your team understand exactly what you are aiming for and get the word out to as many people as possible that you are about to start.

Then the day itself comes. You know that this is a one off opportunity; there will never be another day with the same level of fresh excitement and faith as today. There will probably not be another service that is as easy to invite people to, nor possibly a Sunday where there will be a higher proportion of visitors who are wondering whether to join you or not. It is a day to make count.

When do you launch?

The timing of the launch of a church is very important. It goes a long way to determining the degree of momentum that you will enjoy over the coming months.

It is not unlike the birth of a child. If the child arrives too early, then it struggles to stay alive. If the delivery is delayed too long then it can result in a stillbirth. However, if you get the timing right then great joy ensues for everyone involved.

Launching too early can leave you with too small a group of people in the congregation. There is nothing worse than a small group of people rattling around in a venue that it is too large for them or a church plant with a grand vision but meeting weekly with a small group of people tucked away in a tiny room off the beaten track. If people come in and think that the church desperately needs them in order to survive then they are much less likely to stay.

'We began as a home-based church with twelve adults and five kids. We met in a home for about six months and then launched with twenty-two adults on a Sunday. Looking back, this was too early. The original plan had been to gather about forty people before we launched. The change from meeting in a home to launching on a Sunday is huge and if you are a bit thin on the ground, then the whole focus, along with all of your resources, can switch to making an event happen instead of meeting new people. It meant that by the time people had served in the worship band and others had left the room to run the kids work, I felt like I was speaking to the chairs. It really was a challenge in those first few months.'

Stef Liston, Revelation Church, Camden

Equally, if you leave it too long, then people will become frustrated and de-motivated. The underground phase of meeting in midweek groups can be great fun, but it cannot go on forever.

What are the signs that suggest that you are ready to launch?

1. *You are moving towards the right number of people to provide critical mass*

When you start Sunday meetings you want to be nearing the average number of attendees for a church in your area. This puts you on the map on day one.

2. *You have enough leaders and workers to fill all the roles you need for a Sunday morning meeting*

In most settings these include: a preacher, a worship leader and other musicians, children's workers, welcomers, people to set up and pack away (including displaying signs for parking and toilets, setting up children's equipment, handling the PA, etc), a finance team if you are taking an offering, and a team to prepare and serve refreshments.

3. *You are nearing a time of year when you can expect several months of good attendance to help build momentum*

If you start meeting in May for instance, you are going to go straight into the three lowest months of attendance of the year (typically June to August in the UK). You would be better to wait until September when you know that you will have the maximum opportunity to draw people into the church with the term culminating with the popular Christmas services.

4. *Everyone feels ready to go for it*

A mother does not need to be told that her baby is ready to be born, she just knows! In the same way, there often comes a point when you simply know it is time to launch.

'From January to April, rather than gathering in small groups, we gathered the whole planting team together midweek and had a series of evenings called "Vision Bites" where we worshipped together and taught on our vision and values. We invited Apostolic leaders to come and help lead these evenings and these proved vital in communicating who we were, and building us into a solid, missional, planting team.

In the lead up to the launch we were focused on getting as many people to know what we were doing as possible. We told our families and friends, we had large picture features in the local press and there was an article on the BBC Southampton web page. That helped us to gather people for the first meeting and we invited the local mayor and the press to come along. Over the years I have purposefully attempted to develop a genuine friendship with the media in our area, offering stories and features or comment. Because of this they have been keen to help us when we have something we want people to know about.

We hired a conference centre linked to the university which is located in the main shopping area of Southampton. This was a great location and suited us down to the ground. Whilst being more expensive than some other possible venues, we felt that it would serve our vision most clearly. We wanted to establish something that was in keeping with a city centre ethos to underpin our vision to reach the whole city. Having a well known building on a well known street made it easy to invite people. Quality was also important to us and the building was smart with good audiovisual equipment. This helped us to communicate that we were hoping to be a "good" church right from day one.

On that first launch Sunday, literally as I was getting up to begin speaking, the hundredth person walked through the door and I think the total number ended up at about 104 people on that day. Obviously, we dragged in every man and his dog for that, so it wasn't the realistic state of the church at the launch. But it was our first gathering and we felt like we'd really begun.'

Chris and Jo Kilby, Life Church, Southampton

What must you do before the launch?

1. Find a suitable building

You need to find a building that ...

- ... *is of a suitable quality.* The best rule of thumb, in my opinion, is to aim for a building that the people you are drawing would come to on other social or leisure occasions. You want people to feel at home in the setting. Avoid the extremes of selecting somewhere either too shabby or run down or too upmarket. Find somewhere that the majority of people would normally go to.

- … *is easily accessible.* How will people travel to the venue? How long will it take people to get there? If it is by car, is there suitable car parking around?

- … *is of a suitable size.* You want a building that you do not rattle around in, but which also has some space for growth. Remember that typically you can only comfortably house around two-thirds of the number of people that a venue advertises as their capacity. Make your calculations on this basis to see whether a venue is the right size for you.[2]

- … *is comfortable.* It is worth talking to the owners about cleaning (if the venue is used for Saturday night functions that finish late) and heating (will the heating be on during the winter and will the venue be warm before the first people start to arrive for the meeting?).

2. *Gather your team and explain what you are looking for from Sunday mornings*

Explain how Sundays are going to work and gain the team's ownership. They are going to need to work very hard for the next few months whilst newcomers get to the point where they are ready to help out.

3. *Get the news out that you are starting*

The very best way of doing this is by sharing the news personally with those that you and others in the church plant know. Nothing is more likely to be successful and it is critical that this is your major focus. Remember to lead by example in this. Share with the rest of the church plant who you are inviting and encourage them to do the same.

You may find that there are other ways of reaching people who you would otherwise not get to speak to. These may include:

- Press releases in the local newspapers
- Advertising on local radio
- Direct mail shot
- Literature drop near the venue or in student halls of residence
- Blogging, email and use of websites

You may also want to invite family, friends and supporters from other churches. It helps get things off to a great start to have a really good crowd present.

However, also be aware that if you have too many well wishers then your numbers on week two will be significantly lower, even if there are notably more people than you ever had in the pre-launch phase.

4. *Consider doing a rehearsal*

Remember you only launch once and it is worth getting it right. The best way of ensuring this happens is to do a dry run the week before.

'*Before we launched in London we decided that we would do a rehearsal the week before. It felt a bit funny saying to the people, "Next week we are doing a rehearsal for the real thing" and then asking them to come and pray and worship as normal, but everyone got the hang of it and it worked fine. We also spotted a number of potential problems and were able to get them sorted before our launch the following week when we had (what was for us) a huge number of visitors and newcomers.*'

David Stroud

5. *Prepare your people for the fact that not everyone will come back for the second week and that is OK*

Remind them that the goal is to have more on the second Sunday than they had in the previous stage when they were only meeting in small groups.

Things to remember on the day of the launch

1. *Ensure that you communicate where you believe this church is going*

Cast a vision that others will want to be a part of. Tell your story, explain where you have come from and what you believe God has told you to do. Help people understand what the church is going to become.

2. *Make sure that your team are focused on giving a warm welcome to everyone who comes along*

'When we arrived in Birmingham, one couple who were part of my team went along to three of the larger churches in the city on consecutive Sundays. They were very struck by the fact that on each occasion nobody welcomed them. On one occasion one of them took their daughter into the crèche and stayed with her and nobody else spoke to her for the whole time they were there.

They concluded that there would be one very straightforward way to give people a very positive experience of church: to make sure everyone was genuinely made to feel at home and welcomed well.'

David Stroud

3. *Have a follow up procedure in place*

You may feel that to begin with having welcome cards and a team to follow up first time visitors, as many larger churches do, is either not appropriate or beyond your resources. However, you should nevertheless be clear about how you are going to follow up those who have visited for the first time.

I have always sought to ensure that my key leaders are not only ready to welcome newcomers, but find a way of staying in touch by getting some kind of contact details. I will then ensure that everyone is followed up during the next week.

4. *Make it clear that you are part of* Newfrontiers

Being part of a network gives credibility and will allay any sense of fear or distrust for some first time visitors.

You should also consider becoming a member of the Evangelical Alliance prior to the launch. This also gives credibility and shows that you are part of mainstream evangelical Christianity.

'Be ready to deliver on that first week: worship, sermon, childcare, refreshments, signs. You want to look like the real deal even if it is a stretch!'

Matt Hatch, Mosaic Church, Leeds

'In 2001 Nicky and I moved to Hillingdon with a small group of twenty people. Before we launched we had three groups spread over twelve miles of London. We felt that God was really in this because it meant that there were loads of people over a broad area to reach out to. Ever since we have been focused on filling in the gaps between the groups.

This strategy also meant that we needed to choose a venue that was not surrounded by houses and give ourselves a name that didn't define our geographical boundaries; we didn't want to send a message that we were looking to reach only one neighbourhood within the borough.

In the launch week our small groups distributed 20,000 leaflets at tube stations and libraries, and we took out ads in the local press. We arranged for a crowd from another local Newfrontiers church to join us on the first Sunday, to create a buzz. The following Friday we had a large outreach event with a guest speaker who told his remarkable life and death story of being stung by a box jellyfish.'

Pete Cornford, Crown Church, Hillingdon

Children's ministry

1. *It is important that the children's work is of as high a standard as possible*

If the children enjoy coming to church on a Sunday it makes it a much more attractive proposition for the parents to return.

2. *It is also important that supervision is in line with all the appropriate legislative requirements*

That all workers have been cleared by the Police as not having any criminal record. This creates a sense of confidence for the parents that their children are in a safe environment.

Worship

1. *The most important quality for anyone leading worship is that they are a worshipper themselves and that they are full of the Spirit.*

2. *Bear in mind too that musicians of a reasonable quality attract more of the same, so it is worth using them if you have them.*

3. *Avoid setting the room out in too formal a 'theatre' or 'lecture' style if at all possible*

A horseshoe arrangement gives a much greater sense of community and involvement for people early on.

People will also find it a lot easier to lead in prayer and use spiritual gifts during the worship if the room is set out in such a way that they can easily be heard.

4. *Maintain a balance between the size of the worship band, the volume of the PA and the number of people in the room*

One or two acoustic instruments will work fine with fifty people, but by the time you get to 100 you probably need to be working towards having a more developed band.

Even then, beware that the band doesn't dominate the worship with too great a volume as this tends to reduce congregational involvement which should be high at this point in time.

Preaching

The greatest challenge of preaching in the early phases of a new church is finding the time to prepare. This becomes easier as the church grows and other leaders develop who can take some of the workload. However, in the early days do not feel pressurised to spend too long working on your sermons. Use whatever help you can get from others and develop a team of preachers. Use guest speakers from nearby *Newfrontiers* churches. Do not let the burden of the preparation distract you from gathering people, developing community and training leaders.

* * *

If the launch has worked well you will have really gained momentum. The longer you can keep this sense of being thrust forward the better. In the next section we look more closely at some of the things you can do to make the most of this season.

18

DEVELOPING MOMENTUM

'Given enough momentum nearly any kind of change is possible.'[1]

John Maxwell

'In the days when horses hauled four-wheeled wagons and cars to and fro in the shunting yards of England's railways, it was reckoned that a good horse could pull up to six empties once they were on the move, but could only start one from rest.'[2]

J.I. Packer

'During those first three years ... the gospel seemed brand new, sleepy/nominal Christians awoke with a start and people got converted every week. The air was charged with a kind of electricity. Every decision turned out to be wise. Everyone performed above and beyond their gifts and abilities.'[3]

Tim Keller

There was a terrific sense of unity, excitement and energy amongst the group of twenty-somethings that started the King's Arms in Bedford. We had known each other for a long time, God was already at work amongst us and we had a clear vision for what the church was to become.

Once the church plant began, numbers grew quickly.

Within nine months we had five small groups with around eighty people attending and we then began weekly Sunday meetings. Our first meeting had all the excitement and energy that you might expect from the launch of a church plant.

But that was only the start of things. This surge of energy continued for a significant period of time after the launch as well. For the next nine months we continued to grow quickly. It felt like we were being 'pushed' along by the hand of God. The turbocharged atmosphere became a magnet that drew others in and many of them quickly reproduced the same levels of commitment and contribution that others were already giving.

We felt God was on us in a wonderful way and within eighteen months we were one of the larger churches in the town.

We had enjoyed a season of great momentum. Momentum is of enormous value to any church planter. It enables you to gather more people more quickly and overcome apparent obstacles with ease.

How do we build momentum?

1. Cast a big vision that creates faith and commitment

One of the key ways of creating momentum is to develop a sense that the team are about something much bigger than themselves. They have to be convinced that starting this church was God's idea and that he will therefore provide everything they need.

Telling your story regularly can really help create this conviction. It should involve how you came to start this church, but also where you believe God is going to take things in the future.

2. Live with an urgency about gathering people in the early months

One of the key elements that marks out effective church planters is the sense of urgency they live with when it comes to gathering new people. They understand that momentum is developed by an expectation that there will be new people each time the church gathers together. They understand that this expectation only comes about through new people turning up regularly in the early weeks and months.

The church planter lives knowing that this is his responsibility.

'Our first meeting in Birmingham was in our home on a Wednesday evening and we had seventeen people who joined us on that occasion.

We had a great evening together as we talked about the sort of church we believed God wanted to build.

However, at the end of the evening when everyone had left, Philippa and I looked at each other and I said, "We have had a great evening tonight, but I will feel like dying if we cannot find at least one new person to add to the group by this time next week." I knew Philippa was in agreement, but neither of us had any idea where this person was going to come from!

Nonetheless, God was good to us and the next week there were eighteen of us in the room. We were off to a good start!'

David Stroud

3. Give great energy to gathering people in the early months

Developing momentum is like pushing a heavy goods train up hill – it demands enormous effort to start with, but once it is at the brow of the hill it gathers pace all by itself, and once it is hurtling down the other side it is pretty hard to stop!

This enormous energy and effort to get things going comes from you. As the church plant leader you have to, with all God's grace working in you, give it the 'push' needed to get going. This requires great vigour and ensuring that the energy you give is directed towards the right things.

This 'push' cannot be manufactured, but must come from a God-given passion for lost people and a clear understanding that you must get things going quickly if you are to grow well through the early stages of the church's growth.

'We had a tough time picking up momentum and it probably was not helped by going to Sunday meetings a bit early. What it made us do, however, was to really focus on reaching out and being missionaries to Camden. I had expected people to just start to turn up when we began on a Sunday, but that did not happen. So, rather than waiting for people, God really challenged my heart that we had to go and find them. This has affected the whole church as a result.'

Stef Liston, Revelation Church, Camden

4. *Ensure there is a sense of celebration*

This drive and urgency could easily create a feeling that tasks are more important than people if you are not careful.

Do not forget, therefore, to ensure that there are lots of opportunities for people to play together and celebrate everything that God is doing among you.

We have always looked for every excuse we could find to celebrate victories that have been won. Every time we multiplied a small group we would throw a party to celebrate the wonderful things that had happened whilst that small group had been in existence. Doing this creates a great sense of gratitude for all that God is doing and a sense of awe that we can be co-workers with him.

'On the day that we left Bedford to move to Birmingham, Matt and Pip Hatch came round to see us off. They brought with them a bottle of champagne. As Matt gave this to me he said, "This is to be opened when you see your first person come to Christ in Birmingham." Our good friends understood the power of celebration!'

David Stroud

5. *Make sure there is a sense of fun*

People love being part of a community where they can laugh and have fun.

Make sure that the gathering events you have are the kind of events that you would love to go to yourself. If you are not enjoying them then there is something wrong. The chances are that others will not be enjoying them either.

Laugh a lot and develop a culture where others are laughing too. Don't take yourself too seriously and remember to say 'thank you' to others a lot. As the church plant progresses you might even want to have occasional 'thank you' events to which you invite all those who have worked hard to get the church plant to this place. We have sometimes combined these with some light-hearted 'awards ceremonies' as well.

6. *Give people opportunities for personal growth*

A sense of communal surging forward is representative of many individuals feeling that the same is happening in their own personal lives.

Therefore, constantly keep your eye out for opportunities to help people grow. Faithful people will often play the same role for a long time and your job as leader is to ask the questions they may not be asking like, 'Should you now contribute in another way? What steps do you need to take to keep growing? Who could take your role to release you to work in another area of church life?'

Without this sort of approach people will sometimes lose their passion, burn out or even decide to worship somewhere else because they feel there are few opportunities to grow where they are.

7. *Take risks to help maintain an atmosphere of faith and expectation*

There is nothing that adds to a sense of momentum like a victory won or a risk successfully taken.

This is why it is important to constantly be asking the Lord what your next steps are for the burgeoning community.

Every now and then God will set things before you that other people will regard as impossible, yet you know God is speaking to you about them. It is these risks that are worth taking.

At times, I have deliberately sought the Lord and asked him for a risk to take or a challenge to lay before the church plant in order to keep them stretched and faith rising.

'The early days of gaining momentum in the church plant in Camberley was largely generated by lots of meetings, lots of gatherings, lots of sharing of ideas, vision casting and praying together. The meetings were not always spiritual times. We ate together, had fun and developed relationships. I remember Colin Baron giving me some very helpful advice when we started by saying, "Spend time reading Acts and drink lots of coffee." So that is what we did, particularly during *the first year. After eighteen months we were gathering ninety adults who shared our values.*

In years two and three I realised that to maintain the momentum I needed help to build a stronger leadership team and to appoint elders. Getting the right 'horses' to run with me pulling the 'chariot' was of enormous benefit. After a few years, several of the original leadership team moved on to go and plant other churches, so it was important to have developed a wider pool of core leaders to keep us moving forward.'

Mark Landreth-Smith, Beacon Church, Camberley

When the church plant is full of momentum, leadership is fun and exciting. You don't know who is going to walk through the door next or what miraculous news is going to get shared with everyone.

However, church life is not always like this. It is easier to lose momentum than it is to gain it. Any church planter should be aware of the momentum stealers that can subtly sap the energy and life of the church plant. These are the subject of the next chapter.

19

MOMENTUM STEALERS

'Almost all churches have one thing in common when they first start out: sky high idealism. "We are not just going to change our community or our city or our nation," they cheer, "we are going to change the whole world" ... That is until reality sets in. Over time church leaders and congregations alike are dismayed to learn how much energy it takes to keep the machinery of a growing church moving along ... Slowly but surely that "God can do anything" feeling fades, bold prayers quit being prayed, and the beginning of the end is near.'[1]

Bill Hybels

'The main thing, is to keep the main thing, the main thing.'

There is little more disconcerting for a leader than realising that the momentum the church has been enjoying has started to wane. It may not be that things are going badly. On the contrary, new people may still be joining the church, people might be getting saved and lives being changed, but it is simply not happening as quickly or with the same level of energy or power that it was.

Equally for others, the stories they hear about the momentum other churches are enjoying can seem very distant from their own experience. They have enjoyed slow, steady blessing, but have never known the kind of breakthrough that a quickening of momentum can bring.

In the last section we looked at the positive things that can be done to gain momentum. In this section we look at the other side of the coin. What are some of the mistakes we can make that can steal momentum from the life of the church?

1. Trying to do too many things in the early days

One of the big temptations in the early months and years of a new church is to try to do all the things that the large church down the road does.

The minute you fall into this trap you lose the terrific benefit of focus. Focus enables you to marshal your energies on a few things and do them really well.

'From time to time you may find that people will want you to start new ministries within the church (for example, ministry with the poor, discipleship, counselling, etc), on the basis that "every church does this" or because "the church down the road does such and such".

I have often responded to this request by comparing a large superstore and a local bread shop.

In the large superstore you can buy just about anything: not only food, but coat hangers, televisions, books and flowers. In the bread shop, however, you can get one thing only: bread.

The superstore is what we hope the church will become in due course – able to provide all the different types of ministries that the Bible mentions and which we want to provide for the community.

However, I explain, right now we are much more like a bread shop. A bread shop does not try to do everything. It simply tries to do well the one thing that it does (in this instance, sell bread!). The church should do the same, doing well what it does now. This is probably small groups, Sunday celebrations and reaching out to those who do not know Christ.

In due course, the bread shop might add a deli to the variety of breads it stocks, and later it might add the sale of some vegetables, but it has to grow gradually, adding one line at a time as the previous lines are successful.

In the same way, I encourage people to let the church grow gradually, adding new ministries as the previous ones become firmly embedded in the life of the church and as the church has the people and money available to expand.'

David Stroud

2. *Poor organisation*

Church planters typically prefer to spend their time with people rather than organising things. However, the life of the church plant does need organising as well.

If people do not know where the meeting is or what time it is going to finish they are less likely to turn up. If they do not know what is expected of them as they start to get involved in serving, then it will sap their energy and leave them feeling confused and frustrated.

3. *Becoming predictable*

Momentum creates energy, creativity and faith. Boredom does the opposite. It reduces commitment, enables people to become distracted with other things and causes heads to drop.

As a church planter you should do everything in your power to ensure that boredom does not creep into anything you do. Beware of dull meetings, overlong meetings and community life with little variety to it.

Keep a pace and energy to everything that is going on. Watch your own emotional state. If you become bored then the chances are that others are feeling the same way. Review what you are doing and ask what you need to do to bring back a sense of life and excitement into things.

'We had lots of fun events: dressing up as 007, having drinks at a fancy wine bar and then seeing the latest Bond film; going bowling together; even forming a curling team to experience Scottish extreme sport!'

Matthew Clifton Brown, King's Church, Edinburgh

4. *Difficult or hurting people taking too much of the leaders' time*

You will not have been leading the church plant for long before needy people start asking you for time to counsel or support them. A church plant can be very attractive to people in great need, because a small group of people can give them ready access to the leader of the church in a way that would be much harder in a larger setting.

The problem with this is that these people can easily become a distraction for you. Instead of pouring your time and energy into things that will add to the growth and momentum of the church, you can become deeply involved in complicated and difficult situations that are hard to resolve.

I am not saying this to be heartless or unloving. Rather, I'm motivated by the fact that if you remain focused on the things that will bring you growth and momentum, then you will be able to build a church that is big enough to care for many people in struggling situations.

This can be a particular challenge for those with a strong pastoral gifting for they will feel particularly drawn towards these sorts of people and situations. It can take great self-discipline to resist getting involved, but I would encourage you to be very cautious of giving needy people too much of your time in the early stages of church planting.

5. *Failing to guard the flock from predators*

Jesus warned us that 'wolves' (Matt. 7:15) would come amongst the church from time to time. Church plants can be vulnerable to people who get very involved with a small community and then undermine the leadership or sap the spiritual life from the church.

This can happen in a number of ways:

a. People who constantly criticise or undermine the leadership of the church. They often do this in informal settings, speaking to whoever will listen, and do not take their concerns to the leadership, share them and then leave them to be considered. In other instances, these people pick on the most vulnerable people in the church plant and 'whisper' dissent and division in their ears.

Do not allow this sort of thing to go unchallenged in the church. It can quickly have a very negative effect on what God is doing.

Explain to such people that if they have concerns they should discuss them with you, but you do not expect them to talk with other members of the church in a way that will undermine your leadership or create division.

'During the first year of starting the King's Arms there were a couple of men who started to show up who always wore very sombre and serious expressions. Although they were young and trendy looking, the very sight of them would sap me of energy! I found that they were very critical of many of the things we were doing and they wanted to impose lots of extra rules on the men and women in the church in order that they would stay "holy".

I explained to them that Paul had much to say in his letters about adding extra rules to the gospel and it was never very complimentary, but they refused to listen and were not at all open to reconsidering their position or adopting another point of view.

*After they had been attending for a number of weeks I was told
that they were being very free with their criticism to anyone who
would listen, especially new Christians or people who were particularly
vulnerable. As a result, I asked to meet with them and planned to
explain that I would like them to talk with me (or one of my fellow
leaders) about their concerns, but they should not be doing so to
the new members or people on the fringe of the church who they so
often picked upon.*

*However, they did not show up for the meeting and never appeared
at church again. They obviously anticipated our conversation and
decided they would be happier elsewhere.'*

David Stroud

*b. Men and women who gain some level of leadership in the life
of the church before it becomes evident that they have serious
character flaws or are living double lives.* When sin is exposed
in a leader's life, particularly in a new or smaller setting, it
can have a very negative effect on the whole church plant.
It undermines trust, saps faith and makes many groups
introspective whilst people come to terms with what has
happened.

There is no foolproof method that can ensure this will
never happen, but it does underline the importance of you
(or another member of your leadership team if you have
one) building some level of relationship with people before
they take on leadership roles in the church.

When sin is exposed like this it is very important that
the matter is handled well for everyone's sake. Make sure
you talk with your coach and get advice so that a leader's
sin is dealt with in a sensitive and biblical manner.

*c. Men and women who are not interested in serving, but only
gaining positions of leadership.* Do not ask people to take

leadership responsibility in the church until they have first shown their readiness to serve.

d. Men and women who want you to shape the church according to their vision rather than your own. Watch out for those who see your new church as a way of fulfilling their vision. These people will want to convince you of their own passions and vision at an early stage in their relationship with you and will want you to shape the church accordingly. They are often greatly motivated by these things and are not really interested in serving the church unless these things are in place.

It is important that you are clear on what God has called you to do. Do not be afraid to be explicit with them if you cannot foresee embracing their particular emphasis or passion. Explain to them that if they are going to settle happily with you then they need to have a passion for the church plant's vision. Their goal should be to assist the church in its mission, not to change the church!

e. Those who want to focus on a small minority group within the community. On other occasions you may be approached by those who have a particular passion for a small group within the wider community. This may be a particular ethnic or demographic group that is particularly hard to reach into.

It is easy to feel a real sense of pressure to get involved with a worthy cause and marshal the resources you have to support it. However, unless you feel this is the group of people God has already put on your heart, be very careful that you do not become distracted.

On occasions like this I have asked people to share my vision for the whole of the community. I have told them

that if they will share this with me then I would expect
that, in due course, we will have the strength and maybe
even the specialist skill to reach the group they care so
much about. But, I will explain, we cannot give particular
time or energy to it now – right now we have to build a
church that will serve a much wider cross section of the
community.

How do we regain momentum?

It takes some work to regain momentum if you have had
it and lost it, but it can be done. Thought and prayer is
essential as you analyse where the church plant is at.

As you think through why momentum has disappeared
you may come up with a list of different reasons. Talk them
through with your coach and your fellow leaders and ask
them for further insight. Then, set to work changing things
in each of these areas.

Here are some common reasons why you may have lost
momentum and their solutions:

- You do not have enough leaders to take
  responsibility for the various areas of church life, so
  the training of leaders needs to take on new priority.

- You have stopped meeting new people or providing
  events for people in the church to bring their
  friends and contacts to, so gathering needs to be
  re-prioritised.

- There are some key areas of development and
  growth for you as a leader which need to be
  addressed. Ask your coach and fellow leaders for
  feedback on this and then look to your coach to help
  provide the resources that you need to continue to
  learn and grow.

A loss of momentum can make members of the church feel vulnerable, especially if there has been good growth early on. One of the things that can help prevent this is ensuring that you are building a strong community of men and women who love one another. The next chapter contains some key lessons to help you in this process.

20

BUILDING A
STRONG COMMUNITY

'A new command I give you: Love one another. As I have loved you, so you must love one another. By this all men will know that you are my disciples, if you love one another.'

John 13:34–35

'As apostles of Christ we could have been a burden to you, but we were gentle among you, like a mother caring for her little children. We loved you so much that we were delighted to share with you not only the gospel of God but our lives as well, because you had become so dear to us.'

1 Thessalonians 2:6–8

One of the most enjoyable things about getting a new church going is creating lots of events that provide opportunities for a strong community to start to develop.

We have had numerous house warming's and parties; we have been to the theatre, eaten meals galore and enjoyed picnics, held barbecues and intensely competitive games of touch rugby, ultimate Frisbee and softball; we have drunk wine with friends, danced the evening away on a riverboat and eaten tapas in an art gallery; we have held winter barbecues around a big fire, gone to fireworks parties and drunk mulled wine after Christmas Carol services. It has been out of these events and many others like them that people have started to connect, which is the basis of friendship. Out of this a community starts to develop.

Forming a community is a very powerful thing. I have often marvelled at the way in which the vision, teaching and relationships of this community shape so many people's lives. Some people will find their closest friends in the church you form. Others will raise their children in it and others will grow old in it. Some will look back and say that this community saved their marriage or helped them through the hardest time of their lives. Others will remember it as the place where they grew spiritually more than anywhere else. It is a remarkable privilege to be involved in building the church.

Building a sense of community

'[When a church plant is small your strengths are] community and relationships — that's the best thing you have to offer. You're not going to have lots of programs yet ... but you can do what bigger churches have a more difficult time doing given their size: You can love each other and have fun together and enjoy everybody knowing each other. You can incorporate new people into the heart of the church with an ease you will never have again.'[1]

Steve Nicholson and Jeff Bailey

1. Give plenty of time in the early days of the church plant for people to get to know each other

Exchange stories and have fun. Remember, relationships are the glue that holds people together and so the more time you can spend with each other the better.

'Coming from a large church where it is relatively easy to choose who you get to know and spend time with, it was exciting to find ourselves in a new urban setting intentionally trying to create a new community by building fresh friendships.

We were pretty quickly convinced that building a strong sense of community was going to be crucial to the health of our new church plant.

In the early days we intentionally built community in the following ways:

a. We ate together a lot (or perhaps we just ate a lot!). Food and eating together is such a common theme through the Bible that we simply copied that. Until we reached about thirty-five people in the church we probably all ate together once a week. As the church has grown we've maintained a culture of eating together in smaller groups whenever we can – it's a great way to add new people.

b. We ran events with the express intention of building a wide "fringe" for the church – people who wouldn't call themselves part of the church, but were very happy to come along to different events and get to know people in the church. We held jazz nights, quiz nights, fireworks displays, Mums and toddler groups, community action groups, sports groups, weekends away, local festivals, kids fun days, etc.

c. We prayed together every Sunday evening. This helped us to build a community that was Christ centred and focused on mission. It also gave us another opportunity, particularly for our 20's, to gather and, of course, to eat!'

**Duncan and Gill Hanton, Northwest Church,
Mill Hill, North West London**

2. *Provide contexts in which people can share something of their story with each other*

As people share where they have come from and who they are, relationships form more quickly and friendships start to deepen.

Part of your focus at this point is not only to connect with people yourself, but to encourage them to connect with one another. As things develop, there will be no way that you will be able to be at the centre of every relationship, so you will have to spend more and more of your time introducing people to one another and helping them get to know each other.

3. *Teach about the importance of community*

It is important to show people that what they are experiencing is central to the Bible's view of the church. The New Testament often emphasises the fact that the church is about people and their relationships with one another. It is a family, not an institution.

Talk a lot about the value of loving each other and how others will see Jesus through your love and care for one another.

4. *Work hard on improving your own relational skills and communicating your love and care to everyone you meet*

Avoid superficial techniques that lack genuine affection and learn to become really strong at hosting events, breaking the ice with new people and showing genuine care and love for those who are hurting. Most people can get better at these things simply by focusing on them and making them a priority in their own minds.

I am convinced that we can all learn to listen well, ask questions and remember names and previous conversations. Give attention to these things; those who have mastered them are not simply 'naturals', rather they understand how important these things are and how much we can communicate our care through giving them our attention.

Remember that the way in which you relate to others and care for them will set the tone for the whole community.

> 'The most important single ingredient in the formula of success is knowing how to get along with people.'
>
> Theodore Roosevelt

5. *As a sense of community is developing, there is one particular danger to watch out for*

It is very easy for the community to turn in on itself and forget the world it came to reach.

You will sometimes find that people are so enjoying the relationships they have that they stop reaching out to others. They may still talk and pray about the lost, but they stop actually doing it. As a result, more and more time is spent with the people already in the church plant and less and less with others.

This can kill the church plant!

One of the most important and subtle skills every church planter must develop is the ability to gather new people and build community at the same time. Those who are part of the church plant need to be shaped into a family whilst others need to be constantly brought in.

In our church plants we have deliberately avoided having meetings just for the core group unless it proved absolutely essential. Rather, every meeting was open and we worked very hard to have new people at every event possible. In this way we constantly emphasised the importance of relationships whilst also clearly communicating that we are always going to be growing and new people were always going to be added in.

'When you think about community you should not only think about the people already in your church community, but about those hundreds that God wants to add to your community.'

Mark Driscoll at the *Newfrontiers* Together on a Mission Conference, 2008

'Being spread out geographically we were very intentional about developing community through local cell groups. To highlight the importance of these our mantra became, "Sundays, Cell and Alpha!"

As the leader I taught, thought and planned around these community groups. Using the groups to serve on Sundays helped shift the focus from a midweek meeting to a lifestyle together.

I modelled love and care by having people back for Sunday lunch every week for the first year, demonstrating the value of being together in homes fellowshipping over food.

As a guy working full time alone I would spend about an hour a day making contact with people: phone calls, visiting, emailing, texting, writing notes, etc. This helped nurture care within the initial stages of the church plant.

Prayer meetings were great for stirring our passion for the lost and hearing God speak to us. They were also where we interceded for people in the church and brought a sense of community.'

Pete Cornford, Crown Church, Hillingdon

Pastoral care

It will really help you to have a clear picture of how pastoral care is to be provided before the church plant begins. As a result, you will know how to respond to each request that comes for you to care for those who are hurting or needy in some way.

Whilst it is important to provide appropriate care for others, this must not become your primary focus during the gathering phase of the church plant, otherwise you will not have time to take the church forward and you will not develop a church that will, in due course, be able to care for many.

The following principles should prove to be helpful:

1. *Encourage people to care for one another*

The New Testament has a lot to say about the fact that we should be caring for one another and that care is primarily something we should do for each other (Rom. 12:10; Col. 3:16; 1 Thess. 5:11).

2. *As you release people to lead small groups you can involve them in the process of caring for others*

This is the principle Jethro gave to Moses (Exod. 18:17–23). Any leader will become overwhelmed if every need in the community comes to them, so it is much better if they raise up others to share the load. They are then free to support the new leaders and to handle the really difficult cases that the others cannot manage.

3. *Here are a number of other factors that you should bear in mind as you develop your small groups*

- Make sure that you give attention to your small group leaders to ensure they are well cared for. You will be modelling to them the kind of pastoral care they should be giving to the people in their groups. Remember, that people do what you do, not just what you say.

- Arrange regular meetings with your small group leaders to provide them with support as they care for others.

- Remember that most of your leaders will have neither the time nor the skills to deal with the more complex pastoral situations that will occasionally arise. It is in these situations particularly that they will require your advice and support.

Do not be afraid to speak to your coach if situations arise that you feel are beyond your own skill or experience.

4. *Make it clear, where necessary, that you are not able to provide the sort of intensive care that is required for Christians with deep-seated or long-standing problems*

You simply cannot afford to take time away from your other priorities at this point in time to give this sort of care. If you do, you will never get to build a caring church that will be able to help many in the future.

It can be helpful to liken pastoral care in a church plant to the care you receive in the sick bay on a battleship, rather than in a hospital. In other words, care is important, but an army cannot become over focused on caring for the long term hospitalised. They have other 'units' that are better equipped to provide this care; it is not the role of the front line troops.

5. *Watch out for negative, critical individuals who complain, undermine and distract you and the rest of the people from the task at hand*

Make it clear to people like this, graciously but firmly, that there is no place for attitudes like this in a church plant. It is important for them and for everyone else that they do not continue with this sort of behaviour.

Your small group leaders will also need your support and help to deal with people like this, otherwise they can undermine a group and damage the people within it.

Pastoral crises

A church plant is more vulnerable than an established church and a pastoral crisis can have a very deep effect on the life of a small community. A death, serious illness or marriage break-up can have a massive affect on everyone and sap the life of the church plant.

When these sorts of things hit you early on they call for wise and experienced leadership. Make sure that you get advice from your coach and have them visit the church plant at appropriate times to encourage and strengthen the people.

'Some years ago we visited one church plant that had suffered a great tragedy several months before. The leaders' young daughter had died after a long illness.

The whole church plant of 40–50 people had been deeply impacted by this and, unsurprisingly, they had stopped reaching out to others and become very focused on managing their grief and supporting one another.

As we talked and prayed with the leaders it became evident that the other people in the church had not moved on out of deference to the couple who had lost their daughter.

It was therefore our job to help the church plant get back to the business of planting a church, whilst making space for the parents to continue the grieving process.

In a very powerful and moving time of prayer the parents encouraged the other leaders to take the church forward. They encouraged them to start to gather people, train leaders and celebrate life whilst everyone acknowledged that they still needed some more time to re-orientate themselves to life without their daughter.

This proved to be a key moment in the life of the church and one that led to fresh growth amongst them.'

David Stroud

There is one essential part of any community that we have not mentioned: this is the eldership team who are responsible for it's care. These leaders will bring stability and security to the growing church. We must now look at the process of raising up, identifying and appointing the church's first eldership team.

21

DEVELOPING AN ELDERSHIP TEAM

'To the elders among you, I appeal as a fellow-elder, a witness of Christ's sufferings and one who also will share in the glory to be revealed: Be shepherds of God's flock that is under your care, serving as overseers – not because you must, but because you are willing, as God wants you to be; not greedy for money, but eager to serve; not lording it over those entrusted to you, but being examples to the flock. And when the Chief Shepherd appears, you will receive the crown of glory that will never fade away.'

1 Peter 5:1–4

'Now when I went to Troas to preach the gospel of Christ and found that the Lord had opened a door for me, I still had no peace of mind, because I did not find my brother Titus there. So I said good-bye to them and went on to Macedonia.'

2 Corinthians 2:12–13

When I started the King's Arms I had no other elders and therefore had to build the team from scratch. After several years I was frustrated with the level of progress that had been made and started to cry out to God for his intervention. God answered my prayers in a way that I had not expected and sent me someone from another nation who was ready to become an elder.

It came about as the result of a powerful prophetic word when a team came to minister to us from overseas. The team leader had said to me on arrival that he wondered whether God had spoken to him about one of his team coming to be based at the King's Arms for a season. In the first meeting we had that weekend, one of our church members turned to this man and said, 'You have come here to minister to us, but actually we have got a lot to teach you.' He then went on to suggest that this man should come and be based in the church for a while.

This was not the way we were expecting the meeting to go! However, after further thought and reflection this is exactly what happened. In due course Jeff and I were both appointed as elders. This whole process was a wonderful reminder to me that God is in control and building his church.

One of the most important tasks that any church planter faces is developing a team of leaders around him who, in due course, will be appointed as elders. The first time elders are appointed in any church is an important day. It means the church plant is now clearly beyond adolescence and can stand on its own feet with its own leadership who are answerable to God for the life of the church.

Typically, there will be some mature leaders in the church planting team who will become elders in due course or others will be added into the church plant in the early period who will emerge into leadership. However, there are times when the church planter has to start with very raw material and slowly but surely shape these men to the point where they are ready to become elders. Either way, God is in charge and will bring the right team together.

What are the benefits of an eldership team?

Once elders have been appointed the responsibility for the life of the church transfers from the apostolic team overseeing the church to the local eldership. They are now accountable before God for the life of the church (Acts 14:23; Titus 1:5).

Working as a team of elders carries a number of other benefits:

1. *Teams teach us something about the character of God*

They can be challenging environments to work in and they require love and patience, mutual submission, honesty and trust. In other words, they are places where we grow in love and godliness.

A team that is working well is a great demonstration of what God himself is like (it reflects the relationship, mutual submission and honour that is present in the Trinity) and brings a great sense of confidence and trust to the church as a whole.

2. *Teams can accomplish so much more than individuals*

A team does not rely on one individual and their mixture of strengths and weaknesses. Rather, a team that is working well enables each member to focus on their strengths, knowing that as they excel in the areas in which God has gifted them, so everything under the team's care will grow and prosper.

3. *Team life brings accountability to its members*

Accountability and mutual submission are very important for leaders who are going to last for the long haul. We all need other leaders who will give us feedback and a fresh perspective on how we are living and ministering.

4. *Team life also brings a sense of balance*

It stops any one gift from dominating and brings a measure of maturity as different gifts make their contribution.

5. *Teams make better decisions than individuals*

We all have blind spots and things we miss. None of us have all the bright ideas, so we need each other.

> 'For lack of guidance a nation falls, but many advisers make victory sure.'
>
> Proverbs 11:14

What is the role of an elder?

According to the New Testament an elder's role can be described under the following headings:

1. *He directs or leads the church (1 Tim. 5:17)*

In other words the elders are responsible for ensuring the church knows where it is going and how it is going to get there. They are also responsible for ensuring that church life is conducted appropriately on the journey.

2. *He is responsible for the teaching of the church (1 Tim. 5:17; Acts 6:2)*

Not every elder will be a great public preacher (1 Tim. 5:17), but he must be able to understand the Scriptures and teach them (1 Tim. 3:2) and be able to be part of a team that guards the church against anything that will undermine the truth and promote false doctrine.

3. He is responsible for keeping watch over the church (Acts 20:28)

In other words an elder is to care for the church. This does not mean that he has to do it all himself, but rather he ensures that there are pastoral care systems in place so that everyone is receiving care.

He must also ensure that the church is being run in a godly way. This will include ensuring that the church finances are dealt with appropriately and that church discipline is exercised as required.

He is to pray for the sick (Jas. 5:14).

4. He is to release others into their ministries (Acts 6:1–7)

The role of the eldership team is to direct and lead the church and ensure that the different ministries and responsibilities of the church are being carried out. The role of the rest of the church is to make their contribution to the life of the church as they use the gifts and ministries God has given them to strengthen it (1 Cor. 12:12–31).

What is the role of the team leader?

The team leader's role is crucial to the healthy functioning of the eldership, just as James' leadership seemed to be essential at important moments in the life of the early church (Acts 12:17; 15:13–21; 21:18).

The team leader plays a number of significant roles. These include:

1. The recruiting of the team

Nobody else will go and get the team for you; this is up to you.

2. *Ensuring everyone makes a healthy contribution to the team*

This includes both encouraging the more reserved team members to stay actively engaged and not letting the more extrovert members dominate.

3. *Setting the pace for the team*

Team leaders do this through their personal example, through the way in which they serve the church and contribute to the team.

They also do this by noticing when key changes need to happen in the life of the team. When this is necessary you will need to bring a challenge to the team and then help them make the necessary changes.

4. *Not being afraid to make a clear decision at times when the team cannot agree*

This is one of the most important roles of the team leader. No team will always agree about everything. At times of impasse it is the leader's job to make a decision so that the team can move on.

5. *Developing the other members of his team*

A growing church requires a growing eldership team. As team leader you must constantly be asking how each team member should be growing and encouraging them to develop.

'On several occasions I have sat down with a team of two elders who have wanted to discuss whether a team leader is really necessary. They are keen to point out that they do not have a recognised leader and it does not seem to cause any problems.

I have responded by saying that I can see how it may be possible for the leadership in a team of two to remain undefined in certain circumstances, but as others are added to the team this becomes more difficult. By the time you have three or four members in the team, team life will break down without a team leader, because the team will be run, ultimately, by consensus. Without a main leader everyone has an equal vote. This actually results in the weakest member of the team having the most powerful say, because unless he is ready to move forward then the team cannot get going.'

David Stroud

How do you identify potential elders?

There are a number of qualities to look for in potential elders:

1. Good character

Scripture provides us with two lists of character qualities that are required for elders (1 Tim. 3:1–7; Titus 1:5–9). These lists underline the importance of looking first for godliness, not giftedness, in the leaders that we appoint.

2. Gifting

Elders must be men who have the stature to grasp a sense of how the church is doing as a whole and to carry responsibility for it. They must be experienced and insightful, able to make wise decisions; they must have a track record of fruitful ministry.

3. Availability

Elders need to have the time to devote themselves to their role. It is no good appointing men who, it quickly becomes clear, are not able to attend meetings or carry responsibility for the ministries that God has assigned to them.

Such qualities cannot be identified overnight but become apparent over a period of time as you get to know individuals and their families and watch them conduct themselves in the life of the church.

How do you develop an eldership team?

The very best training for developing an eldership team is to have been a part of one yourself. Books and other training resources can be of benefit, but involvement in the life of a team will teach you things that you will not learn any other way.

If you have not been an elder in a previous church or at least sat in on the meetings of an eldership team, then I would recommend that you ask your coach whether he could arrange this for you as part of your ongoing training whilst getting the church started.

Here are some principles to bear in mind as you seek to develop a team of elders in your church:

1. *The appointment of elders should be made by the laying on of hands of the apostolic team along with other existing elders (Acts 14:23; 1 Tim. 4:14)*

It is very important to involve apostolic ministry in this process. Let them guide you if you have not been this way before and make sure there are opportunities for them to get to know each member of your team.

2. *In the New Testament, leadership is typically recognised after it is clear that God has already anointed someone to do the job (Acts 6:3; 20:28)*

In other words, the appointment is a recognition of what the Holy Spirit is already evidently enabling them to do.

As a result, you should be looking for a clear demonstration that this individual has the gifts and abilities required, by the fruit that has already been borne from their ministry.

3. Scripture warns us against rushing this process (1 Tim. 5:22)

It is always harder to ask someone to step down than to not appoint them in the first place. Therefore, there is real benefit in being thorough in the process leading up to an appointment.

'In the early phase of church planting we sometimes had ten volunteers sit in on our weekly meetings. It felt very much like "all play", even though everybody knew I was the pioneering leader. This flat and open structure helped to develop huge ownership; people felt empowered, they learned about leadership and they responded with the best of their time and money.

Later we developed a core team of six, but we focused on building a well run, well led church. This gave me time to observe the character, competence and capacity of these leaders and to get a feel of the team chemistry.

I probably brought some people too quickly into that original group, and painfully discovered later that they either lacked the necessary character or they did not want to respond to me as their leader. Time allowed the former to step off the team and the latter to get involved in church planting.

After about four years, two other potential elders started to clearly emerge. My wider leaders also recognized that God's hand was on them and we began a year of focused training in which we involved Dave Harper (who was overseeing the church) as well, before the three of us were appointed.'

Howard Kellet, Hope Church, Manchester

4. Eldership is, by nature, a relational role

You are a father to the church. As a result, the people must feel that they are connected with a prospective elder and that there is a good level of relationship present.

The reality is that some will know them better than others, but they must have enough exposure to the whole church (at least in a church of under 200 people) so that everyone feels well connected to them.

5. An appointment should have the full support of the people in the church

Clearly, it is foolish to ask people to follow elders that they do not have confidence in.

This means that there needs to be some level of consultation before final decisions are made regarding appointments. I have always been through this process informally to begin with (talking with key leaders privately to get their opinion on whether we have identified the right person/people) and later talking with the whole church and, where necessary, asking them for feedback.

'Raising up elders in a church planting process has not always been straightforward. My experience is that it is worth taking your time over. On several occasions I have seen excellent men who have ministered effectively and who the church have loved, who have found themselves out of their depth when moving into an eldership setting. On both occasions I was profoundly glad that we had a testing period (facilitated through a leadership team) to ease this process and help us realise that it was not going to work before (rather than after!) an appointment was made.

This process can take 3–5 years in a new church planting situation. Do not worry or panic. Keep developing people and challenging them to take their next step, but let the process take it's course.'

David Stroud

A model for the appointment process

Here is an outline of a process you can take potential elders through on the way to appointing them. As you will see, it is a process which gives a number of opt out points for you or the potential elder along the way, if either of you feel this is not developing as you had hoped.

Bear in mind that you do not need to take every step. Sometimes it is clear to everyone that someone should be an elder and you can move ahead to appointing them pretty quickly. However, it is worth giving care and attention to the process.

1. *Watch someone develop as you give them different areas of responsibility*

Watch how they minister and see whether they are effective and whether people feel loved and cared for by them.

2. *Invite them to join you (and the team if you have one) to talk about issues that affect the whole church*

You can keep it very informal if you wish. Simply let them sit with you on a few occasions and see how it works out.

3. *Form a leadership team*

Explain to the church that you are creating a 'leadership team'. Remember to make it clear to everyone that you are working with this team to oversee the church and make sure that its formation has their full support.

Explain that a leadership team does not function with the same authority that an eldership does. Rather, it functions on behalf of those who have authority in the church. A leadership team gives you an opportunity to see how people are likely to function in an eldership type situation, without actually making the appointment.

Let everyone know who you have invited to join. Ask them for feedback. It is important that you gain their ownership as part of this process. Allow a period of time to see how things progress.

4. *If things continue to go well and you know the church are supportive you can then move forward to an eldership appointment*

Getting the most out of team meetings

An effective eldership team ensures that their meetings are enjoyable and productive. Unless clear thought is given to how meetings are going to run, it is very easy for them to become de-motivating and frustrating, rather than envisioning, productive and satisfying! Here are some guidelines:

1. *Start on time and finish on time*

It can be frustrating for people who work hard to arrive on time, only to find that others are not ready to start.

2. *Make sure you are clear when the eldership team (or leadership team) are going to pray together*

Will you make prayer a significant feature of every meeting? Or will you have particular times set aside for praying together? Decide on a definite approach.

3. *You will probably benefit from having some meetings that are less structured, where you can go with the flow of the discussion and be more creative*

It is often helpful to investigate the 'what if' scenarios that can present themselves as you talk and pray together.

These open ended times provide a good opportunity for thinking through the challenges and opportunities that are most likely to present themselves over the next few years.

4. Other meetings can have timed agendas, with each item having a finish time

This helps if you have a lot to get through and not too long to get it done.

5. Ensure that the issues that require more creative thought or are demanding in other ways are dealt with at the start of the meeting

You will get the best thinking out of people when they are fresh. As the meeting progresses you can turn your attention to more straightforward or organisational matters.

6. Ensure that everyone is contributing

This is particularly important when a team starts to meet and people are finding their feet. Some might need to be drawn in and encouraged to comment from time to time, whilst others may need clear direction so that they do not dominate.

7. Make a note of any agreed action and who is responsible for ensuring it is done

Start the next meeting by reviewing this action list.

Building an effective eldership team

Here are a few things to bear in mind as you shape the life of your eldership team:

1. *Teams should play together as well as work together*

Create opportunities to eat meals together, relax together and enjoy life with each other.

2. *Teams should learn together*

Do not just spend time working on the business of the church. Have times when you take a step back and learn together: work through a book together; ask someone to come in and do some training with you; go on a leadership development course or conference; spend time reflecting together on what you are currently learning.

3. *Develop a team with a mixture of gifts and strengths*

When you cannot find the person with the gifting you want, make sure that you are developing the leaders you have and then pray to the God of the harvest to send the right person to you.

*   *   *

The chapters that follow are particularly relevant to elders who, alongside their other responsibilities, will be involved in building relationships with other churches, helping leaders from other churches come into the church and ensuring that the financial and legal elements of church life work properly.

22

BUILDING RELATIONSHIPS WITH OTHER CHURCHES AND WELCOMING FORMER LEADERS INTO THE CHURCH PLANT

'James, Peter and John, those reputed to be pillars, gave me and Barnabas the right hand of fellowship when they recognized the grace given to me. They agreed that we should go to the Gentiles, and they to the Jews.'

Galatians 2:9

'I have given them the glory that you gave me, that they may be one as we are one: I in them and you in me. May they be brought to complete unity to let the world know that you sent me ...'

Jesus prays for the church in John 17:22–23

Before starting a church I have often gone and visited some of the evangelical church leaders in the area. I have done this because I wanted to introduce myself, build some relationship with them and assure them that I am not wanting to attract people from their church, but to reach those who do not know Christ.

Typically, I have been warmly welcomed and it has not been unusual for good friendships to stem out of these early meetings. However, on other occasions I have been told that there is either no need to plant another church in this location or that I should only really do so in a very specific (and normally particularly challenging) area of the town.

I always withstand the feeling that I should pack my bags and head home at this point. In almost every area of the UK, nine out of ten people do not go to church. There must be room for plenty more churches pretty much everywhere if these churches focus on the lost!

I am not suggesting we should not listen to leaders of other churches. That would be foolish. We should always be open to the advice of others, but our primary job is to discern what God is saying and ensure we are obedient to him.

This sort of experience has proved to be a salutary reminder to me as well. If others want to plant near my base, then I too should ensure that I am warm, open hearted and welcoming as they seek to add their contribution to what my church is already doing in the area.

Britain needs new churches. Let's do our best to get the job done. Let's welcome and support others in their endeavours to do the same and follow God's hand as he guides us into other areas of the nation as well.

Relationships with other churches

As we seek to build good relationships with other churches in our area, remember that:

1. *We should seek to genuinely honour the whole body of Christ*

We must remember that no one church has a monopoly on God's blessing and there are always things that we can learn from others.

Our love for them and desire to honour them should be reflected in our attitudes and the way in which we speak about other churches, whether in public or private.

2. *Important to introduce yourself to other evangelical church leaders when you begin the process of starting a new church*

This should be done with humility and warmth. You should welcome opportunities to pray together and fellowship as they arise.

3. *Do not take it personally if you do not receive a warm welcome!*

New churches can often seem threatening to existing congregations and their leaders. Remember that God has sent you and that he will bring the fruit. He is the builder of churches and nobody else.

In the meantime, persevere at building a warm relationship wherever possible. It is amazing what a change there can be in the relationship as other leaders get to know you and find that you are not trying to take lots of their people into your church.

'The news that we were planting Hope Church had a rather mixed reception with some other churches in Salford. I invited myself to a leader's gathering and tried gently to explain that we were after lost people, not their people, and that every church was once a church plant. One vicar responded to this by saying, "We were here a long time before you came and we will be here long after you are gone." Another church leader felt this was a little harsh and bravely invited me to speak on Sunday at his church. I gladly accepted.

Although a man of real grace, he introduced me with the line, "We have invited the opposition this morning." I responded by saying, "The opposition in this city is alcoholism and addiction, violence and *debt, loneliness and broken families, unbelief and sin." I felt the forty or so gathered in that chapel warm to me. It felt like the first breakthrough.*

I have determined always to speak positively about other churches and avoid the competitiveness that is so rife. Trust takes time to build, but now I meet to pray with leaders across the city.'

Howard Kellett, Hope Church, Manchester

4. How should one respond if people want to join the church plant from other churches?

Ask them to go and speak with the leadership of their current church and seek to leave in good relationship.

If necessary, talk with the church leaders themselves about any outstanding pastoral concerns they may have. If Christians coming to you from another church have genuine character problems or serious pastoral issues it is worth knowing ahead of time.

Receiving experienced leaders from other churches

Former church leaders coming from other settings can be a real blessing. They can be a source of strength and experience as well as a 'safe pair of hands' when you need someone to help pastorally or to teach at a time when you are not available.

Equally, they can be more challenging to lead than others in the church because it takes time for them to adjust to a new role where they are not actually leading the church and are not necessarily close to the centre of the action.

As a result, it is particularly important that you give former leaders and elders of other churches some personal time as they start to get involved in the church. Give them a warm welcome, but do not avoid raising issues with them as your relationship begins to develop. You want to find the right niche for them that enables them to be fulfilled in their new setting and which maximizes their contribution to the life of the church.

Here are some things that are worth considering:

1. *Try to gain a clear picture of their strengths and weaknesses and their leadership history up until now*

Not every leader is the same. Ask them about where they have led, what they have done, what has been successful and where the personal challenges have lain for them.

2. *Identify and discuss the differences in theology and values between the new church plant and their previous setting*

This is particularly important if they are coming from a denominational background or a different stream of churches.

It is important for them that they understand what you are trying to do and why you are doing it this way. It is worth spending time explaining the particular values and emphasis that you are seeking to build into the new church plant. This will also give you some idea of the degree to which they are ready to embrace the things that God has put on your heart. If they are not prepared to make necessary changes they will continue to operate out of their old paradigms and value systems which will limit the amount of responsibility you can give them.

'We had a number of senior leaders who came to the church plant during the first few years. They can be a great resource, but invariably they have firm views regarding how things should be done. This was made more challenging by the fact that their church background was often quite different from ours.

As a result, I wanted to make sure that they were happy coming under my leadership. I felt it was very important to be clear on expectations, aspirations and roles. They also had quite a lot of unlearning to do!

Keys to making it work were being secure in my own leadership, giving them the appropriate respect, and building a strong, robust relationship that enabled us to have difficult conversations without causing them to back off.'

Jonathan Bell, Churchcentral, Birmingham

3. *Clarify what their expectations are in joining you*

Are they happy to simply serve you and your vision or are they looking for a position of leadership? Do you sense that there is an unhealthy need to lead that is masking insecurity and the need to 'be someone'?

Are they ready to serve you and your vision or do they want to add to it, shape it or develop it? Are they clear that they are joining the church to serve your vision, not to try to adjust it in some way? Are they looking for a special relationship with you or are they prepared to be a part of the church on the same basis as everyone else?

Be wary about creating 'special access' for former leaders who do not want to lead but would like to be a 'special adviser'. There does not seem to be any precedent in the New Testament for people who have influence in a church without also serving in it.

'A leader from a large Newfrontiers church moved house to join the church plant. He had been employed full time by the church he was at for a number of years and had begun to feel God speak to him about moving to a church plant. In order to move to be with us he gave up his full time employment for the church and went back to full time work in the community. He moved his kids' schools; he also paid a high price financially, as our city was far more expensive than where he came from. But he came with an attitude that simply said,

"God has called me and my family here and I am willing do anything you ask me to do."

What impressed me most was that he did not try to transfer his status as a leader to the church plant, but simply rolled up his sleeves to serve. It never seemed to faze him that he had come from a position in a much larger church and was now simply a member of a church with a leader who was younger than him, and in a much smaller situation.

This man and his family have been a major gift to the church plant and a blessing to us. He is now employed by us and part of our leadership team. His example in being willing to lay everything down to follow God's call is a shining light to many.'

Anonymous

....
.. ..
.. ..

23

SUPPORTING YOURSELF WHILST CHURCH PLANTING

In the past many *Newfrontiers* church planters have received financial support from their home church and sometimes from the apostolic team as well. As a result, they have not had to work in secular employment in the initial stages of the church plant.

However, increasingly churches have been started with the leader initially being in full time employment. Over time they have scaled this work back (where possible by working part time for the church and part time for another employer) until they have, eventually, worked full time for the church.

Some leaders who have been in full time ministry for some years find it hard to imagine how one could both hold down a day job and gather people at the same time, but studies carried out in other nations have shown that it makes no difference to the speed at which the church plant gets up and running.

In fact, there are a number of advantages of remaining in secular employment in the early stages of church planting:

1. It reduces the need to get the church plant going quickly

One of the big pressures for those who start by working full time for the church is to develop things quickly enough so that the church can support them before the money runs out.

If you are not careful, this pressure can lead to a hasty approach to decision making and create a feeling of 'drivenness' in the church plant. Conversely, having the leader in secular employment enables the church plant to develop at it's own pace in a natural and unhurried manner.

2. It gives the church planter daily opportunities to connect with people in the community

Given that the greatest need of any church planter is to meet people who are not part of the church yet, finding a job where you meet lots of people is an ideal complement to evenings spent leading small groups and training leaders.

3. It enables the church planter to stay in touch with the world of work and the challenges of being a believer in this context

The church planter's experience of work will inform their leadership, their preaching and their training of others and enable them to be more sensitive to the pressures and opportunities that others live with every day.

4. It costs less money

More churches can be planted more quickly using this model, because it is not reliant on substantial amounts of money up front.

'One of our greatest church planting challenges was to find meaningful work that would not only pay the bills, but also help us get to know people in the community.

Our sending church kindly gave us three months salary and then we were left to fend for ourselves. However, it actually took six months to find work. Most people get jobs through their relational networks, yet we didn't know anybody in Leeds and sadly my ministry experience counted for very little in the marketplace.

Desperate for anything, I finally applied for a sales job with a utility company in their call centre. I had stayed clear of such jobs, knowing they asked for long hours, paid very little and offered little in the way of potential friendships and job satisfaction. Yet we needed the money to survive.

Despite the difficult work situation I managed to work four long days each week — that left me two more days per week for church planting, plus evenings. God provided for us in miraculous ways and we actually received and gave away more money than at any other time in our lives.

I stayed with that company for eighteen months until the church was ready to release me full time. Though it was hard work, it helped me connect with people, understand the pressures of full time work and took the pressure off starting something too quickly.'

Matt Hatch, Mosaic Church, Leeds

When do you start working for the church?

As the number of people in the church plant increases you will get to the point where you simply cannot get everything done if you do not take some of your working day to do it. This is a good indicator that you need to consider giving some time to the church. You will certainly find this is the case once you have started weekly Sunday meetings. The requirements of sermon preparation and the other work that Sunday church demands will require more than you can provide by simply giving time in the evenings and on Saturdays.

This of course, leads to the whole question of how you develop a healthy attitude towards giving in the life of the church and it is to this that we now need to turn.

24

FINANCIAL AND LEGAL ISSUES

'"Bring the whole tithe into the storehouse, that there may be food in my house. Test me in this," says the LORD Almighty, "and see if I will not throw open the floodgates of heaven and pour out so much blessing that you will not have room enough for it."'

Malachi 3:10

'Remember this: Whoever sows sparingly will also reap sparingly, and whoever sows generously will also reap generously. Each man should give what he has decided in his heart to give, not reluctantly or under compulsion, for God loves a cheerful giver. And God is able to make all grace abound to you, so that in all things at all times, having all that you need, you will abound in every good work.'

2 Corinthians 9:6–8

After a year of regular meetings on a Sunday we had outgrown our central London venue and were preparing to move to a wine museum that had some good space for meetings. As we looked at the costs that would be involved and the steep increase in weekly hire costs we realised that we would have to take a big offering to cover our outgoings.

This provided several challenges. Firstly, everyone needed to pray about what they were going to give. Secondly, the leaders had to ensure they had the inner strength and confidence to stand unflinchingly before the people, present the challenge and pray for God's provision!

Over the next few weeks we taught on what the Bible says about regular giving and special offerings. We prayed and asked God for £50,000 and approached the day with a mixture of excitement and nervousness.

You cannot imagine our delight when the total offering came in at £94,000! This was followed, the next week, by an email from someone in the church saying that they wanted to top the offering up to £100,000 and that the money was on its way. God had been very good to us and provided for us with more than we had even asked for.

Asking people to give money is not something most of us think about when we feel the call to church planting, yet it is an important part of leading God's people. So is ensuring that the financial and legal issues of the church are well administered. It is important to demonstrate that we are dealing with these matters with diligence and integrity, as well as looking after other matters that we tend to think of as more 'spiritual'.

In this section we will look at some of the important principles of raising and managing money, as well as other important financial and legal aspects of running a church.

Talking about money in the early stages of church planting

1. Before the church plant begins it is worth having conversations with each member of the church planting team

Ask them to consider giving from the start of the church plant. You will probably find that most of the team will be expecting to do this anyway and your conversation will simply act as a prompt to set them going.

Make sure that you have a bank account open and that standing order and Gift Aid forms are available. You want to make the most of the money that will be given from day one, so you need to be organised in this respect.

'One of our core couples started tithing immediately when they joined us and their tithe alone meant I could go part time when we launched the church in Leeds.'

Matt Hatch, Mosaic Church, Leeds

2. *Giving can be a sensitive issue in the early days of a church plant as you are starting to win people to your vision*

You should be aware of this and not rush people into giving before you know they have really bought into what you are doing.

That said, you should not hold back from making an open and direct appeal when appropriate. Be sensitive to where others are at, but do not become awkward or embarrassed about raising an issue that is important for the church and for every person's own growth in God.

Where possible avoid making public appeals for regular giving until you have more than one small group. When you draw the groups together is a natural time to talk about financial issues. This bigger setting enables you to talk about such issues naturally, without anyone feeling awkward.

Consider taking an offering each time you meet in this setting. Also make standing order and Gift Aid forms available to people who have just joined you so they can begin to give regularly.

Money principles

1. *Teach the church well on giving*

Do not be afraid to preach on money, the Bible has a lot to say about it. However, make sure that your teaching on this, as in all other areas, is full of grace. The appeal to give to God's work should always be rooted in thankfulness for what God has done for us and never because of a sense of obligation. If you find yourself using words like 'ought to', 'have to' and 'must' then it is likely that you are straying away from a grace-filled approach and it is worth pausing to re-evaluate.

2. *Make sure that you teach on every area of money that the Bible covers*

It can be tempting to talk only about what the Bible teaches about giving, but the Bible also has things to say about saving, spending and managing our money. If you are to develop a well rounded, mature church then it is important that you are covering each of these areas and not only talking about giving.

3. *Make sure that you are giving generously and regularly yourself*

There is an important spiritual principle here: as the leader, you set the spiritual temperature for the life of the church by the way you live and the things you do. This works not only for the things that others can see you doing, but also for those things that are done in secret like your prayer life and giving. Set the pace for generous giving in your church by the way in which you give yourself.

'I remember announcing that we were going for a big offering one time. I knew that this would stretch everyone's faith and I have to confess that I was not entirely confident that we were going to get the amount that we were going for.

As the day of the offering drew closer, I was still not at a point of peace about it. I found myself thinking about what we would do if we did not get all the money we were praying for – not exactly a faith-filled place to be!

Then my wife happened to mention that she felt we should be personally giving twice what we had planned to give. It was a massive amount for us at that time, but I instantly knew she was right and that this was God's voice.

The next few minutes were very instructive: as soon as I decided in my heart that we should give that amount, I also knew that the church would hit the offering target. My personal obedience was followed by a gift of faith that the church would reach its target, as indeed it did.

I had learned again that a leader's first job is to be obedient to the voice of the Holy Spirit and that, somehow, when it comes to giving, there is a link between the leader's response to God and the response of those who follow.'

A church planter

4. Remember that people give best to a compelling vision

People give to vision much better than they give to a particular need. When you speak or preach about the need for money always connect it to the vision that God has given you. This will focus people's attention on God's future plans for the church and cause them to give sacrificially to his work.

5. There may be occasions when it is appropriate to take special offerings for particular projects or needs within the life of the church

Such offerings can be wonderful opportunities to see God provide in amazing ways. However, make sure that you do not have them too often, that you give people plenty of notice beforehand so that they can prepare themselves, and always explain what you are planning to spend the money on before you take the offering.

Administering church plant finances

1. *It is important to ensure that the finances are well run (2 Cor. 8:19–21) because ...*

   - *... it is the right thing to do.* The Bible has a lot to say about the importance of managing our responsibilities with integrity. Ensuring the church's finances are well run is an important example of this.

   - *... it builds trust.* People are, rightly, sensitive to how money is handled in a church setting. As a result it is important that we are able to demonstrate that we are managing the finances well. Trust is a very valuable commodity for any leader to have; it causes people to follow them wholeheartedly.

   - *... the Charity Commission is giving increasing attention to how churches and charities administer their finances.* This is because some churches have not taken their legal obligations seriously. It is very important that we give sufficient attention to this area of church life to ensure that everything is being done well within the requirements of the law.

2. *It can be beneficial for another larger church to run your finances for a while during the start up process*

This works particularly well where the sending church continues to serve the church plant by running their finances for a period or where a larger regional base is able to serve church plants in their area in this way.

There are several advantages to this:

- It saves you having to administer the finances at a time when you need everyone you have to gather new people.
- It gives you time to find qualified people who can help you with the finances.
- It enables you to claim Gift Aid (see below) from the start of the church plant.

For this to work effectively it needs to be a church that is well resourced so that the managing of the church plant money is not too onerous for them. They would simply ensure that all money given goes through their books whilst keeping the church plant money separate for the church plant's use. Your coach should be able to advise you on this.

'Once I had to pay our weekly offering into the bank. I travelled into the city and on the way to the bank visited our meeting venue, a 17th Century church building in the middle of the city. Rather naively I put my bag down to check our equipment was stored correctly and upon my return discovered it had been stolen, along with our offering! I resolved in my mind to delegate both jobs (checking our gear and depositing the offering) as soon as humanly possible!'

Matt Hatch, Mosaic Church, Leeds

3. Draw up a budget before you start the church

This should show you how much money you will need on a month by month basis, what you will be spending it on and when.

This may be hard to do initially because it is difficult to judge exactly how things are going to go over the early months. Your first budget may have an element of guess work about it, but do not let this put you off. You can revise it as you go on, but simply going through the process will prove to be of great value and may cause you to ask some questions and see some challenges that you had not really focused on until now.

4. *You should also ask whoever is managing the money to supply you with monthly reports on income and expenditure and the amount of cash you have in the bank*

This enables you to have a good idea how the church plant is doing financially and whether there are issues that you need to be praying about or addressing.

5. *Ensure that you have proper systems in place for the counting, banking and administration of the money*

This not only demonstrates that the finances are being well managed, but prevents people from being accused of poor administration or, worse, of fiddling the books!

If you or your other leaders do not have experience of managing financial systems then make sure you get advice and help from a qualified individual.

'I remember being in one pioneering situation and being shocked to see the person who had collected the offering going back to their seat and pouring the money out of the offering basket into their bag. Then, at the end of the meeting they marched out of the door with the bag on their shoulder!

I knew the leaders well enough to know that it was very unlikely anyone was being dishonest, but I was concerned that there were no proper procedures in place for the handling of money.

I would have hoped that two people would have counted the money and verified the amount in writing (with signatures) before the money left the building and that there would then be an agreed procedure for banking the money with further checks that the amount banked corresponded with the amount that had been counted after the meeting. This would have ensured that everyone was safe from being falsely accused of mishandling money and it would have given a sense of confidence to the church plant that such matters were taken seriously and dealt with properly.'

A church planting coach

Getting organised: the legal bits

1. *It is beneficial for the church to become a recognised UK charity*

This gives credibility when a new church is starting which is important.

Various trust deeds are available for you to look at on the website, www.ukchurchplanting.org but it is also important to get professional advice on this.

2. *Bear in mind that Gift Aid is available in the UK on all gifts given by UK tax payers*

This results in the Government returning most of the basic rate of tax to the church on gifts given by UK tax payers. However, this benefit is only available if you are an established charitable trust. This should be a good incentive to start the application process as soon as you start the church plant.

3. *As you start your own charity you will be required to appoint trustees*

These are very important appointments because these men and women have significant levels of responsibility in the life of the charity.

Ideally you are looking for people who have experience of legal and financial matters, have good 'business sense' and are people of faith.

They should also be loyal and faithful members of the church who are happy to look to the elders for the leadership of the church whilst also understanding and fulfilling their responsibilities to the Charity Commission.

They will work closely with the eldership on legal and financial matters.

If you have not appointed trustees or worked with a board of trustees before then it is worth discussing the dynamics of this with your coach who will be able to help and advise you further.

Appendix A

WHAT SORT OF CHURCH ARE WE TRYING TO BUILD? PRINCIPLES FOR NEW TESTAMENT CHURCH LIFE

This manual has focused on the things that you need to do to get a church started. However, it has assumed an enormous amount in terms of what the Bible lays down as essential principles for church life.

Below I have listed some of the characteristics that are fundamental to healthy church life. We are seeking to build these into every *Newfrontiers* church that we start.

1. *The priority of the local church*

The local church is the instrument that God has designed to further his kingdom. His people are his passion and great love. Therefore, we are to give our time, energy and money to the building of the local church. As we pursue God's mission it is the church that should be our prime focus and greatest priority.

2. *The mission of the local church, is …*

- … *to win the lost:* reaching those who do not know Christ is of paramount importance. Therefore, everything the church does should be infused by this drive and focus (Matt. 28:18–20; Acts 1:8).

- ... *to care for the poor:* Jesus spent much of his time with the needy and marginalised. The local church is to care for those on the fringe of society, the isolated and outcast (Matt. 25:34–46; Luke 4:18–20; Jas. 1:27).

- ... *to shape culture:* the church is to shape wider culture as it releases time and energy for members to be involved in influencing society according to God's values (Matt. 5:13–16).

- ... *to plant churches:* every church should be aiming to plant further churches with the assistance of apostolic ministry (Acts 19:10).

- ... *to go to the nations:* God's intention is to bless the nations of the world. Each local church should reflect that by sending men and women across the world to be involved in winning the lost, caring for the poor, shaping culture, planting churches and going to the nations (Gen. 12:1–3; Matt. 28:18–20; Acts 1:8).

3. *The leadership of the local church*

The church is directed by elders. Male elders and other leaders win the hearts of people through their servant hearted leadership and care. They are free to lead and have clear authority, but this is not imposed or demanding (1 Tim. 5:17; 1 Pet. 5:1–4).

The church is served by apostles, prophets, evangelists and pastor teachers. These ministries are still to be exercised today and these gifts strengthen and equip local churches. They also keep the church's eyes lifted to the greater mission field beyond their local situation and provide a context in which people can go to the nations (Eph. 4:11–13; Acts 14:26–28).

4. *The life of the local church, will include ...*

- ... *a commitment to Scripture:* the church must be
  shaped according to the principles of Scripture and
  have a deep dependence and reliance on Scripture
  (2 Tim. 3:16–17). This will be demonstrated by
  the time given to preaching, the way in which
  biblical truth under girds the songs and prayers
  used in worship and the consistent reference to
  what Scripture says when corporate and personal
  decisions are made (Col. 3:16–17; Matt. 6:33–34).

- ... *the grace of God:* God's undeserved favour is
  not only available for us as we come to Christ, but
  is the nature of our relationship with God for the
  rest of our Christian lives as well (Rom. 5:2,17;
  Eph. 2:8–10). This is an incredibly liberating
  dynamic that not only fills our lives with joy, but
  also shapes the feel of the local church including
  the way in which leaders lead and the way people
  relate to one another (Rom. 12:6; Rom. 15:7; 1 Pet.
  5:1–4).

- ... *life in the Spirit:* every church should be looking
  for ongoing powerful experiences of the Spirit. This
  begins on a personal level with being baptised in
  the Spirit (Luke 11:9–13; Acts 1:8) and leads to the
  use of the gifts of the Spirit in worship and ministry,
  looking to hear prophetic direction for the life of
  the church and experiencing other supernatural
  outbreaks of God's love and power in the life of the
  church and the wider community it is ministering to
  (Luke 9:1–6; 1 Cor. 14:1).

- ... *the importance of relationships:* natural, positive,
  caring relationships are part of the essence of biblical
  church life. Care comes primarily from each other,

but is guided and shaped by those who pastor the church (Eph. 4:32, 5:21; 1 Thess. 5:11; Heb. 3:13; Acts 20:28).

Appendix B

MISSION, VISION AND VALUES WORKSHEET

Andy Moyle
Gateway Church, King's Lynn

Some preliminary questions to work through ...

- What Scriptures have grabbed you?
- What prophecies have been spoken over the plant?
- What has God been saying to you personally?
- What have you found frustrating about church that you wish to change in this new setting?
- What have you found out about the area you are seeking to reach?
- What would be the headline and content of a newspaper article about the church after five years?
- What would the church look like if God made all the resources available that you needed?

1. Write a mission statement

A memorable, short statement of why the church exists. (Examples: 'To know Christ and make him known'; 'Changing lives with God's love, grace and power'; 'A place to begin, believe, belong'.)

2. *Write and re-write your vision statements*

- 30-second version to answer questions like, 'Why have you moved here?' and 'Why are you starting a church?'

- 3-minute version for more interested people at the end of a gathering event.

- 30-minute version for preaching.

3. *Test the vision*

... on your wife, core team and anyone you meet!

- Is it clear?
- Is it concise?
- Is it inspiring?
- Is it achievable?
- Is it measurable?

4. *Focus the vision*

You may find that the vision naturally leads to a series of goals. (These may be one- or two-year timeframes in the early days and three- to five-year timeframes as the plant matures into a church.)

It may be helpful to write these goals down. Remember it is the vision not the goals that motivates people, so do not be tempted to set unrealistic goals. You must have faith that the goals are achievable. Huge goals may be motivational, but will subsequently rob you of momentum if you fall a long way short of them.

At this time you may wish to clarify ...

1. *Your core values*

The way in which you will do church life (culture more than doctrine, e.g. 'We value growing people over being professional'; 'We seek to live the life we are inviting others to lead.')

2. *Your core beliefs*

The non-negotiable doctrines that govern church life. It may help to adopt a statement of faith from a mature church with a strong theological foundation.

FURTHER READING

Every church planter should start to build up a library of books. This should include theological reference books (dictionaries and commentaries), works of theology, teaching and Christian biography. However, for the sake of this reading list, I have resisted the temptation to try and cover all these categories and have limited myself to a few books and articles on church planting, leadership and associated issues.

These resources come from a broad range of backgrounds and consequently, should be read carefully and with discernment. They will stimulate your thinking, but you should not assume that just because the book is listed here that I recommend everything in it.

Church planting

Keller, Timothy J. and J. Allen Thompson, *Church Planting Manual* (Redeemer Presbyterian, 2002).

Malphurs, Audrey, *Planting Growing Churches for the 21st Century* (Baker Books, 2004).

Nicholson, Steve and Jeff Bailey, *Coaching Church Planters* (AVD United States, 2001).

Stetzer, Ed, *Planting Missional Churches* (B&H Academic, 2006).

Wagner, C. Peter, *Church Planting for a Greater Harvest* (Regal Books, 1990).

Church Planting in the City

Keller, Timothy J., article entitled 'Planting a Church in the City'. www.redeemer2.com/themovement/ issues/2004/dec/citychurchplanting.html

Keller, Timothy J., series of articles entitled 'Ministry in the New Global Culture of Major City Centres', parts 1–4:

- www.redeemer2.com/themovement/issues/2005/ may/ministry_in_globalculture.html
- www.redeemer2.com/themovement/issues/2005/ fall/ministry_in_globalculture_II_p1.html
- www.redeemer2.com/themovement/issues/2006/ winter/ministry_in_globalcultureIII.html
- www.redeemer2.com/themovement/issues/2006/ spring/ministry_in_globalculture_IV.html

Keller, Timothy J., article entitled 'A Biblical Theology of the City'. www.e-n.org.uk/1869-A-biblical-theology-of-the-city.htm

Schaller, Lyle E., *Center City Churches: The New Urban Frontier* (Abingdon Press, 1993).

Leadership

Clinton, J. Robert, *The Making of a Leader* (NavPress, 1998).

Greenslade, Philip, *Leadership: Reflections on Biblical Leadership Today* (Crusade for World Revival, 2002).

Driscoll, Mark, *Confessions of a Reformission Rev* (Zondervan, 2006).

Hybels, Bill, *Courageous Leadership* (Zondervan, 2002).

Marshall, Tom, *Understanding Leadership* (Baker Books, 2003).

Maxwell, John, *The 21 Indispensable Qualities of a Leader* (Thomas Nelson, 1999).

Maxwell, John, *The 21 Irrefutable Laws of Leadership* (Thomas Nelson, 1998).

Maxwell, John, *Developing the Leaders Around You* (Thomas Nelson, 1995).

Maxwell, John, *Developing the Leader Within You* (Thomas Nelson, 1993).

Smyth, P.J., article entitled, 'The World Needs More Elders' http://godfirst.co.za/resources

Evangelism

Gumbel, Nicky, any of the materials that support the Alpha Course. http://uk.alpha.org/

Hybels, Bill, *Just Walk Across the Room* (Zondervan, 2006).

Hybels, Bill and Mark Mittleburg, *Building a Contagious Church* (Zondervan, 2001).

Preaching

Haslam, Greg, *Preach the Word!* (Sovereign World Limited, 2006).

Stott, John, *I Believe in Preaching* (Hodder & Stoughton Religious, 1998).

Church life

Devenish, David, *What on Earth is the Church For?* (Authentic Media, 2006).

Virgo, Terry, *God's Lavish Grace* (Monarch Books, 2006).
Virgo, Terry, *Restoration in the Church* (Cityhill Pub, 1989).
Virgo, Terry, *The Tide is Turning* (New Wine Press, 2006).

ENDNOTES

Chapter 1

1. Timothy J. Keller and J. Allen Thompson, *The Church Planter Manual* (New York: Redeemer Presbyterian Church, 2002), p. 29.
2. Stanley Grenz, *Theology for the Community of God* (Cambridge: Broadman & Holman Publishers, 1994).
3. Statistics from – World Urbanization Prospects: the 1999 Revision, prepared by the United Nations Population Division.

Chapter 2

1. Kenneth Grahame, *Wind in the Willows* (illustrated edn; Wordsworth Editions, 1998 – ISBN 185326122X, 9781853261220), page 76.

Chapter 3

1. John Maxwell, *Leadership 101* (Nashville: Thomas Nelson, Inc., 2002), p. 11.

Chapter 4

1. Rick Warren, *The Purpose Driven Church: Growth Without Compromising Your Message and Mission* (Grand Rapids: Zondervan, 1995), p. 178.

Chapter 5

1. Robert Greenleaf, Hamilton Beazley, Julie Beggs and Larry C. Spears, *The Servant-leader Within: A Transformative Path* (Mahwah: Paulist Press, 2003), p. 54.

Chapter 8

[1] Steve Nicholson and Jeff Bailey, *Coaching Church Planters* (Stafford: US Association of Vineyard Churches, 2001), pp. 53–54.

Chapter 12

[1] Howard Taylor and James Hudson Taylor, *The Story of the China Inland Mission* (Morgan & Scott, 1894), p. 480.

Chapter 13

[1] Charles H. Spurgeon, *An All-Round Ministry* (Charleston: BilbioBazaar, 2008), p. 227.
[2] Geraldine Taylor, *Behind the Ranges: The Life-changing Story of J.O. Fraser* (Singapore: OMF International (IHQ) Ltd, 1998), p. 192.

Chapter 14

[1] Terry Virgo, from his blog 5th July 2007, http://www.terryvirgo.org

Chapter 17

[1] Steve Nicholson and Jeff Bailey, *Coaching Church Planters* (Stafford: US Association of Vineyard Churches, 2001), p. 130.
[2] The advertised capacity normally assumes a 'lecture theatre' layout. This is placing the chairs very closely together and using the length of the room. In practice, people may be squashed together in this type of format, but they will live with it for a one off event. However, church services need more space for the worship band, space to enjoy refreshments afterwards and enough distance between chairs so that people do not mistakenly hit each other during the worship!

Chapter 18

[1] John Maxwell, *The 21 Irrefutable Laws of Leadership* (Nashville: Thomas Nelson, 1998), p. 200.
[2] J.I. Packer, *A Passion for Faithfulness: Wisdom from the Book of Nehemiah* (Wheaton: Crossway Books, 2000), p. 88.
[3] Timothy J. Keller and J. Allen Thompson, *The Church Planter Manual* (New York: Redeemer Presbyterian Church, 2002), p. 15.

Chapter 19

[1] Bill Hybels, *Axiom* (Grand Rapids: Zondervan, 2008), p. 56.

Chapter 20

[1] Steve Nicholson and Jeff Bailey, *Coaching Church Planters* (Stafford: US Association of Vineyard Churches, 2001), p. 140.